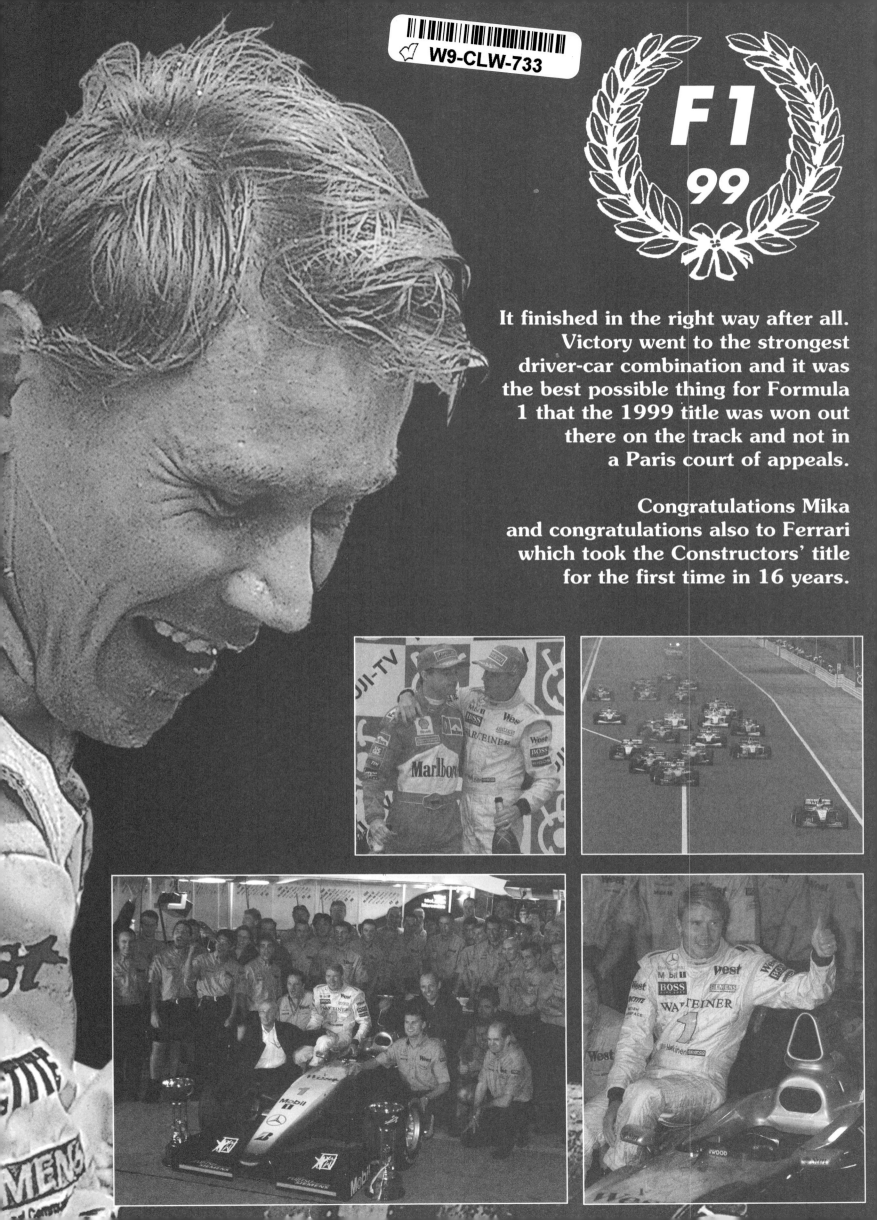

F1 99

It finished in the right way after all. Victory went to the strongest driver-car combination and it was the best possible thing for Formula 1 that the 1999 title was won out there on the track and not in a Paris court of appeals.

Congratulations Mika and congratulations also to Ferrari which took the Constructors' title for the first time in 16 years.

Fotografia *Photography* Fotografie	**Bryn Williams**
Disegni tecnici *Cutaways* Illustrationen *Illustraties*	**Paolo D'Alessio**
Realizzazione grafica *Graphic realization* Grafische vormgeving	**Diego Galbiati**
Coordinamento tecnico *Technical coordinator*	**Ermenegildo Chiozzotto**
Traduzioni *Translations* Übersetzung *Vertaling*	**Julian Thomas, Olav Mol, Nicolaus C. Koretzky**
Fotolito *Colour separations* Reproduktion *Fotolitho's*	**Servoffset - Milano (Italy)**
Stampa *Printing* Druck *Druk*	**Alfa Print - Busto Arsizio (Italy)**
Realizzazione *Editorial production* Herstellungskoordination *Redactie en samenstelling*	**SEP Editrice - Cernusco s. N. (Milano - Italy)**

Printed in Italy - November 1999

© 1999 SEP Editrice - Cernusco s.N. (Milano - ITALY)
ISBN 88-87110-17-4

© 1999 English Edition - Ebury Press - London
ISBN 0-091-87169-7

© 1999 North American Edition - Voyageur Press - Stillwater, MN
ISBN 0-89658-485-2

© 1999 Nederlands Taalgebied Ars Scribendi BV - Harmelen
ISBN 90-5495-324-1

Si ringrazia
AUTOSPRINT
settimanale di automobilismo sportivo leader in Italia,
fonte inesauribile di informazioni e dati statistici ripresi per questo libro,
Daniele Amaduzzi e Actualfoto (Bologna-Italy) per il materiale pubblicato
nel capitolo "50 anni di evoluzione della F1"

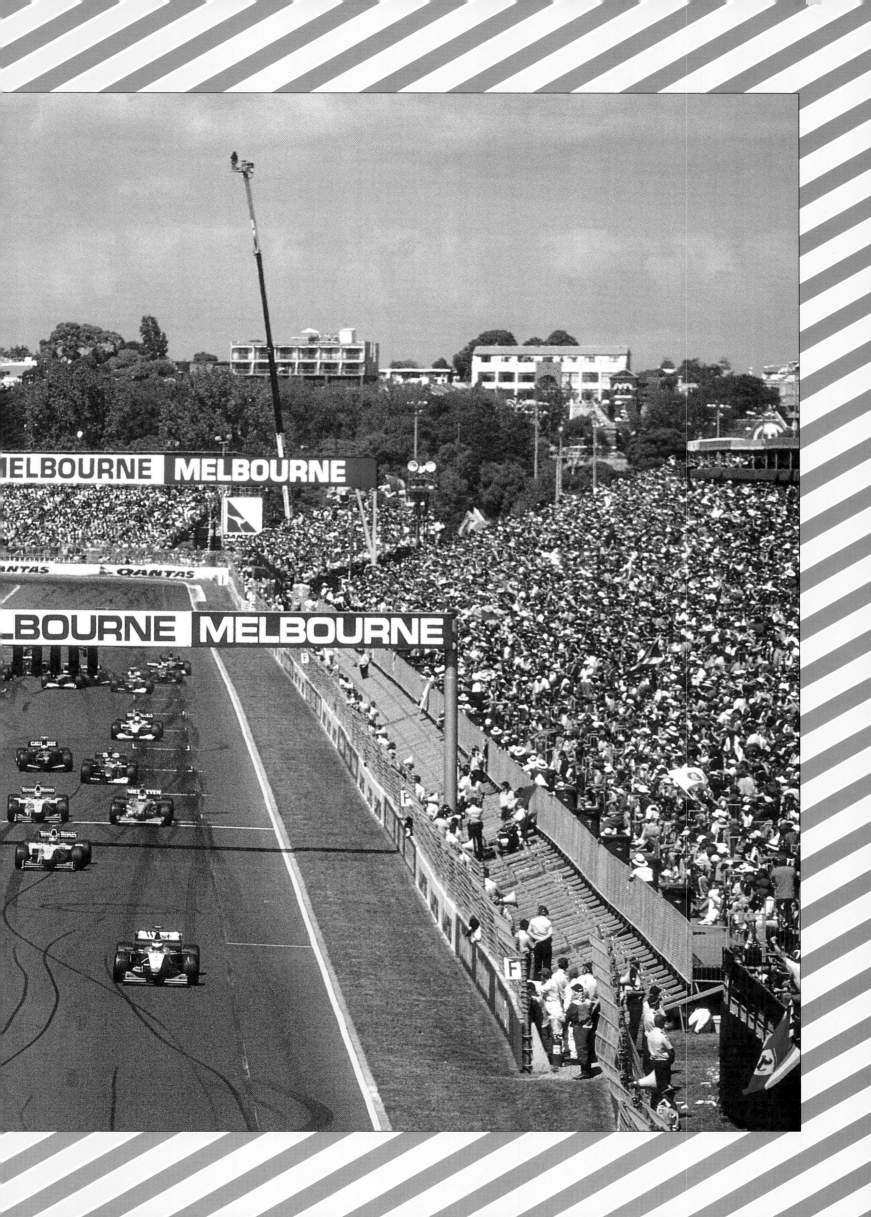

NS
Castrol
Castrol
FUJITSU
Schumacher
auto
motor
sport
nfield
FUJITSU
Winfield

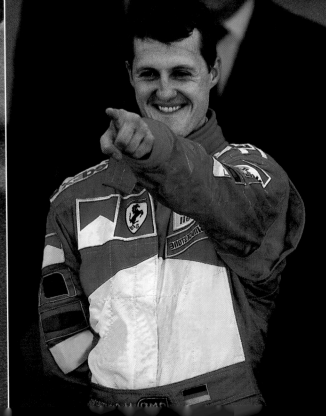

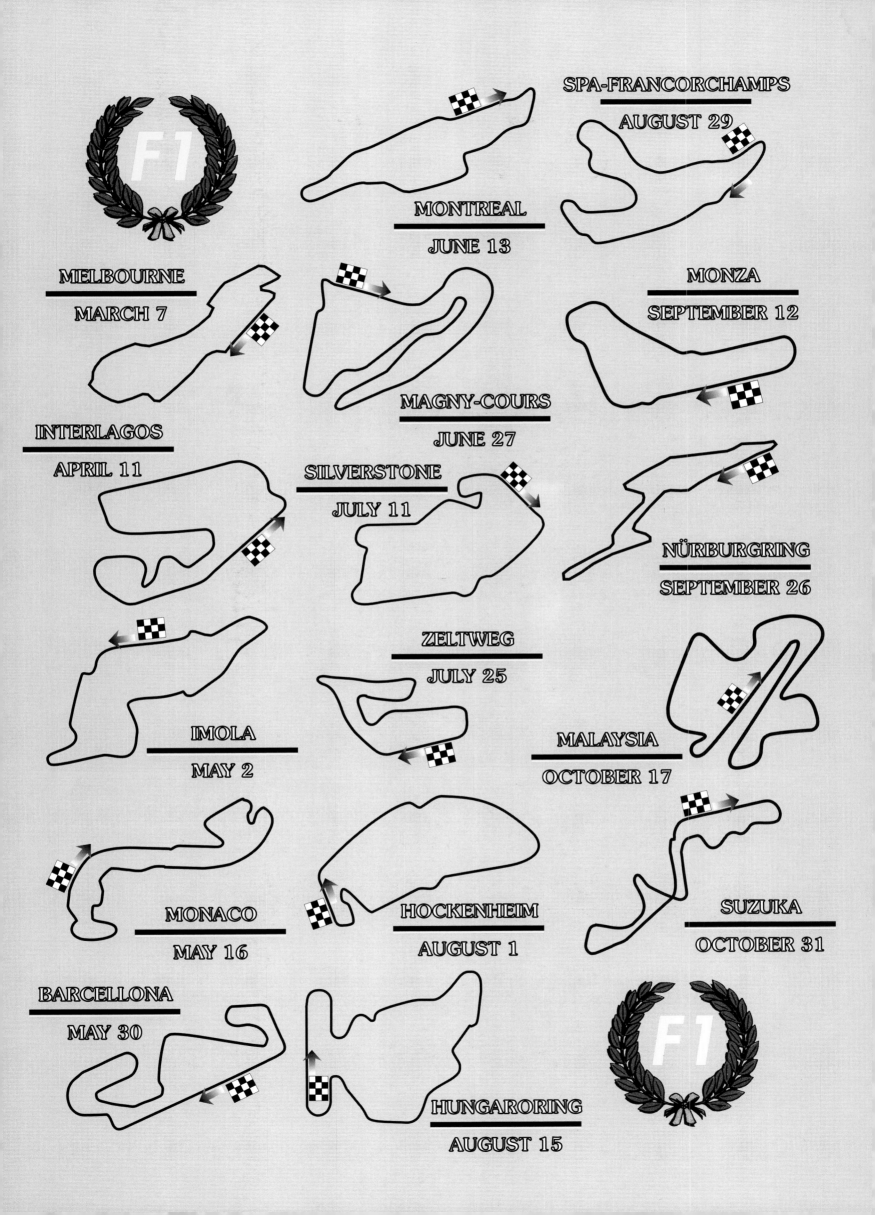

F1

SPA-FRANCORCHAMPS
AUGUST 29

MONTREAL
JUNE 13

MELBOURNE
MARCH 7

MONZA
SEPTEMBER 12

MAGNY-COURS
JUNE 27

INTERLAGOS
APRIL 11

SILVERSTONE
JULY 11

NÜRBURGRING
SEPTEMBER 26

ZELTWEG
JULY 25

IMOLA
MAY 2

MALAYSIA
OCTOBER 17

MONACO
MAY 16

HOCKENHEIM
AUGUST 1

SUZUKA
OCTOBER 31

BARCELLONA
MAY 30

HUNGARORING
AUGUST 15

F1

FORMULA 1 CALENDAR 1999

January 25

The new Jordan 199, together with drivers D. Hill and H.H. Frentzen, is unveiled in London. The engine is a 10 cylinder Mugen-Honda.

January 29

Ferrari's new challenger for the '99 championship is presented at Maranello. All 450 members of the Prancing Horse team are present on the stage.

March 7

• Eddie Irvine (Ferrari) wins the Australian GP. Ferrari has not won the first GP of the season for 10 years (1989 Brazilian GP - Nigel Mansell).
• Damon Hill's 100th GP.

March 26

Ten years ago Johnny Herbert made his F1 debut with Benetton at the Brazilian GP and finished 4th.

April 11

Mika Hakkinen (McLaren) wins the Brazilian GP. This was the Finn's tenth victory in F1. France's Stephane Sarrazin (Minardi) makes his F1 debut.

April 13

Harvey Postlethwaite, genial designer and gentleman, died in Barcelona at the age of 55. His many successful cars included the Wolf WR1 which won on its F1 debut with Jody Scheckter in 1977.

April 29

BAR and Honda sign a deal for the 2000 championship. Honda also becomes a partner in BAR.

April 30

The BMW-Williams makes its debut. The 10 cylinder German engine was tested by Jorg Muller at the Miramas circuit near Marseilles.

May 2

• M. Schumacher (Ferrari) wins the San Marino GP.
• M. Salo makes his 1999 debut for BAR.
• Sauber celebrates its 100th F1 GP.
• Five years ago, A. Senna died in a crash at Imola (1st May 1994). The weekend had begun with another tragedy in which R. Ratzenberger (Simtek) lost his life.

May 13

Forty-nine years ago (13th May 1950) the first GP of the modern era was held. It was called the European GP at Silverstone (England). The winner was G. Farina (Alfa 158).

May 16

• M. Schumacher (Ferrari) wins the Monaco GP in Montecarlo. With his sixteenth victory for Ferrari, Schumacher overtakes Niki Lauda who won 15 for the Prancing Horse team.
• The US GP is presented at Indianapolis. It will be held on 24th September 2000.
• Rubens Barrichello celebrates his 100th F1 GP.

May 30

• Mika Hakkinen (McLaren) wins the Spanish GP in Barcelona.
• Williams celebrates its 400th GP in Spain.

June 10

Ford announced the purchase of the Stewart F1 team. The two founders, Jackie Stewart and his son Paul, stay on in the team as President and Executive Director.

June 12

The Le Mans 24 Hrs race gets underway. It ends with victory for the Dalmas - Martini - Winklehock BMW, managed by G. Berger.

June 13

* Mika Hakkinen (McLaren) wins the Canadian GP at Montreal. Jean Alesi celebrates his 35th birthday in Canada and Jackie Stewart his 60th.

June 23

The FIA presents the 2000 Formula 1 calendar. The championship gets underway in Malaysia on 20th February and concludes in Japan on 8th October at Suzuka.

June 27

- Damon Hill announces his retirement from F1.
- Mercedes celebrates the 100th GP for its engines (24 victories).

July 7

Eddie Jordan confirms to the press that H.H. Frentzen has renewed his contract with the team for 2000.

July 9

Exactly ten years ago, Jean Alesi made his F1 debut at the French GP for Tyrrell in place of Michele Alboreto. He finished fourth in a race won by Alain Prost.

July 13

Ferrari announces that the 33 year-old Finn, Mika Salo will replace Michael Schumacher until the German returns behind the wheel.

July 14

Damon Hill, who had announced his immediate retirement a few days before, went back on his decision and said he would continue until the end of the championship.

August 1

McLaren-Mercedes officially announced it had renewed its contracts with Hakkinen and Coulthard for 2000.

August 7

Michael Schumacher undergoes a second minor operation on his leg to help speed up his recovery. The German driver will probably return to F1 at Monza.

August 20

Forty days after his crash, Michael Schumacher gets back into a Ferrari for a test session at Mugello (Italy) and completes 65 laps.

August 24

Team Prost announced its line-up for the year 2000. Jean Alesi will be flanked by Nick Heidfeld, 1999 Formula 3000 champion.

August 26

Jordan signed the 25 year-old Italian driver, Jarno Trulli, a 'veteran' of 46 GPs, on a two-year contract.

August 26

Mika Salo will replace Jean Alesi at Sauber in 2000 after the Finn signed a two-year contract with the Swiss team.

September 1

In a press conference shortly after a brief test at Monza, Michael Schumacher announced that he would not be racing at Monza or the Nurburgring.

September 4

Gabriele Rumi, Minardi's leading shareholder, is 60 years old. The founder of Fondmetal in 1970 had already taken part in F1 with Osella.

September 4

The 29 year-old Brazilian Rubens Barrichello will be Ferrari's second driver in the 2000 world championship.

September 14

Eddie Irvine will be Jaguar's first driver in the 2000 world championship. In the picture the presentation of the new Jaguar-Ford Team.

September 26

First win in F1 for Stewart with Johnny Herbert at the Nürburgring, where Jackie Stewart won the final Grand Prix of his racing career in 1973.

October 15

Almost 100 days after his incident at Silverstone, Michael Schumacher returns behind the wheel of his Ferrari at the Malaysian GP.

October 17

Triumph for Ferrari in the Malaysian GP with Irvine first ahead of Schumacher, but the celebrations didn't last long because the two Ferraris were disqualified!

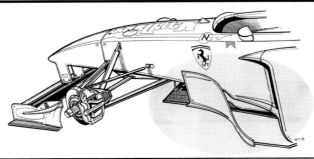

October 23

Ferrari's disqualification was overturned on appeal. In Paris the sporting authorities confirmed the result of the Malaysian GP: 1st Irvine, 2nd Schumacher.

Paddock Focus

New F1 arrivals

Two Spanish drivers and a Brazilian were the three new faces in the Formula 1 circus at the first round of the 1999 season. What was more important was the return of Spanish drivers to F1 after a gap of 10 years and the forgettable experiences of Sala and Campos at Minardi.

Riccardo Zonta, a 23 year-old Brazilian from Curitiba, came to F1 after gaining experience in McLaren and Mercedes. With his team-mate Klaus Ludwig in 1998 he won the International GT Championship but in that same year was also McLaren tester, thus accumulating considerable experience with F1 cars. On loan to BAR, in 1999 he lined up alongside former F1 world champion Villeneuve; a vastly experienced team-mate in a team that was about to start its adventure in F1.

Marc Gené, 25 years old from Sabadell in Spain, instead arrived at Minardi 'with a briefcase full of dollars' from Telefonica, but in the winter tests proved himself to be not only a worthy driver, but also a serious and competent tester. A university graduate in Economics in England, Marc Gené is the brother of one of F1's missing talents: Jordi Gené, who a few years ago was considered to be a natural talent but who had to leave F1 due to lack of sponsors.

Pedro De La Rosa, the oldest of the 'rookies' at 28 years of age, came from Barcelona and arrived at Arrows thanks to the backing of Repsol. In 1998, again for Repsol, he was signed as test-driver by Jordan. On his debut in Australia, De La Rosa drove intelligently, controlling a race that at the flag earned him 6th place and an important point for Arrows in the constructors' championship.

Stephane Sarrazin was the 23rd driver to join the 1999 F1 circus. He stood in for Minardi's Luca Badoer at the second race, due to the injury to the Italian driver in testing at Fiorano (Maranello).
Sarrazin's was not an easy debut; on a difficult track he had never seen before and with a car which was not exactly right for his size (over 1.80 metres in height, 75 kg in weight).
The 25 year-old Frenchman had originally been signed as Prost's test-driver for 1999.

Formula 1 curiosities

It is a well-known fact that the tobacco multinationals, the major sponsors in F1, are not allowed to advertise their products in some countries due to strict anti-smoking laws.
What is less well-known is that the top teams must organise themselves in a particular way to deal with these restrictions; not just regarding livery on the cars and the drivers' suits, which can be seen by everyone, but everything else.
Just imagine 100 people (team manager, engineers, mechanics, personnel, PR, etc.) going to every Grand Prix where tobacco advertising is not allowed.
A T-shirt … or even a sock with the logo of the cigarette company worn by mistake can (and did!) lead to a massive fine for the team.
In order to prevent this from happening, teams have a special department which prepares team gear before each GP, with or without logos.
Each team member is given a sealed bag containing everything that must be worn in that GP. Everything is washed, ironed and labelled with the name of each member. Hundreds of these 'packages' must be multiplied by the number of Grand Prixs and even test days.

Spanish Formula 1

Drivers or super-athletes?

For some time now Spain has been spoken of as a major player in Formula 1, after a long absence of drivers, engineers, etc.

The interests at stake are in fact quite high. Spain has a rapidly-growing economy and there are already a number of big-name sponsors in F1 such as Repsol and Telefonica.

King Juan Carlos is a keen fan of sport and a great believer in it as a promotion vehicle for his country. Recently he was guest of McLaren and during the Spanish GP even had the chance to try out all the thrills of F1 in the McLaren twin-seater driven by Martin Brundle.

Then there are the drivers, and in particular De La Rose who has proved to be a worthy 'rookie', even behind the wheel of a not exactly competitive car such as the Arrows. With his sixth place on his F1 debut in Australia, De La Rosa scored Arrows' first points in the '99 championship.

Formula 1 numbers

Two cars and two drivers for a two hour show is all that the general public sees. But what goes on behind the scenes of a top team in F1?

• About 100 people follow each GP for a top team.

• 8 spare engines are usually prepared and taken to each GP.

• 4 large trucks are required to transport the cars, the spare parts, the engines, refuelling equipment and the pit garage structure.

• 3 or even 4 motorhomes are available for drivers, team personnel, VIP guests and press.

Niki Lauda was probably the first F1 driver who had a personal trainer, an expert in physical and nutritional preparation. This came about towards the end of the 1970s and it wasn't a coincidence that these choices were made by a driver, who was so attentive to little details, such as Niki Lauda, who went on to win three World Titles.

If Niki Lauda can be considered the forerunner, then Michael Schumacher is certainly the driver who has made physical training and nutritional care a style of life.

Schummy is followed like a shadow by Balbir Singh, his massager and expert in sports nutrition, but his real passion is physical training in the gym.

Virtually everyone knows that in his villas in Switzerland and Norway, Michael has had a gym built complete with the most recent and sophisticated training equipment and with the collaboration of Technogym, which today is supplier and sponsor of Ferrari.

Not many people however have had a close-up look at the extraordinary van built by Technogym, fitted up as a

mobile gym for the two Ferrari drivers, Schumacher and Irvine.

The van is present at all rounds of the championship and is made up of a 60 sq m gym as well as a relaxation room and a separate bathroom complete with shower.

This technological wonder cost a total of US$ 600,000.

All the pieces of equipment in the mobile gym are fitted with a small computer, programmed with the exercises and the weights calculated for each driver.

What is the reasoning behind all this?

Today it is absolutely essential that drivers have high-level athletic preparation because they have to deal with sudden braking and centrifugal forces caused by high cornering speeds and the tremendous forces especially on the neck and the shoulders.

To deal with the vibrations on the steering wheel, due to the rigid suspension, specific preparation is required for the arms, the wrists and the hands.

Finally aerobic capacity must also be continually kept high with specific running machines.

The latest Technogym creation is a simulator that faithfully reproduces a F1 cockpit, allowing the driver to fit his own shape seat and carry out exercises to strengthen the muscles most used when driving.

Driver transfer market ...

Just like every year, Montecarlo marks the start of the driver 'transfer market' for the following season.

Damon Hill indicated that he was close to retiring, while at Ferrari, despite an excellent start to the season, rumours were going around that Irvine would get the 'thanks but goodbye' treatment. F1 journalists were all tripping over themselves trying to find secret manoeuvres behind every little detail.

Barrichello was seen chatting to Todt ... Irvine said goodbye to Dennis ... In an interview Schumacher praised Alesi ... Every meeting, glance or remark seemed to give birth amongst journalists to an endless series of possibilities, retainer fees and plans for the year 2000.

As usual, Eddie Jordan moved around the paddock with a sly grin on his face that appeared to send a series of messages to those working in the F1 circus. In the past it was Jordan who was the genius at 'launching' new talent or, in the case of Hill and then Frentzen, 'relaunching' their careers.

One thing is certain however about Jordan: the Irishman has always managed to gain something from the transfer market.

• In the photo, external view of the van and the new simulator that reproduces a F1 cockpit.

• In the drawing, plan of the Technogym van for Ferrari with equipment.

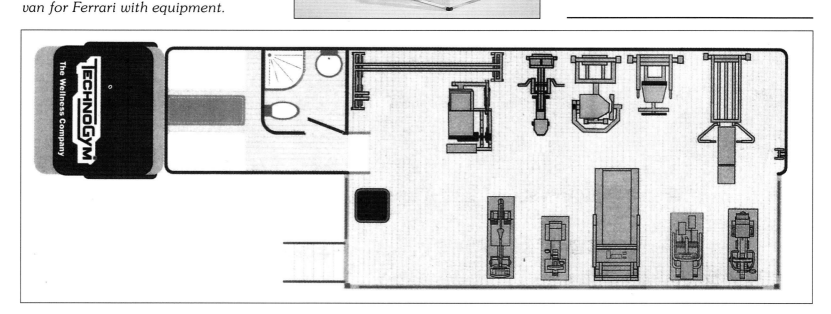

... & team transfer market!

Bernie Ecclestone is not a man who likes to go back on his decisions or appreciates changes in plans and strategies.

He must have been rather disappointed therefore when he learnt of Honda's decision to abandon the idea of becoming the 12th Formula 1 team and to join forces with BAR as partner and engine supplier. The 'Boss' had decided on 12 teams and 12 it must be. Who will be the 12th member of the F1 Circus?

At the moment the only manufacturer keen on entering F1 appears to be Toyota, which is more attracted by the idea of saving money by purchasing an already-existing team, than creating one from scratch and entering the championship.

History teaches us that it is not easy to create a team from scratch and that eventual failure can cause incalculable damage to a major manufacturer in terms of image and publicity.

It is possible to start from scratch (Jordan for example) and get amongst the top teams, but getting involved with major structures and names (Honda's and Yamaha's experience in the past) does not always produce good results.

Driver transfer market part 2

With Schumacher's incident in Great Britain, Eddie Irvine became Ferrari's number 1 driver. In theory, his position in the table meant that he was also in with a chance of winning the world title. For the moment therefore 'the Irvine problem' for 2000 appeared to have been put to one side, even though it seemed that Stewart (now Ford) had made him a massive offer for next year. Ford was determined not to play second fiddle in the driver transfer market for 2000 and was making a number of massive offers which, even though if not successful, would certainly lead to driver fees going up.

Paddock rumours reported that

Hakkinen had been offered 20 million dollars, Coulthard 10 million and Irvine 12 million. How would the teams respond to these offers?

The Zanardi enigma

In January Frank Williams presented the Italian driver to the press with declarations to the effect that 'we chose Alex Zanardi for 1999 because he is determined, fast and a winning driver'. This was true because he had proved it in the United States, winning the CART title for two successive years, '97 and '98, enthralling US fans with his performances.

His duels with Michael Andretti and Al Unser Jr., who had called him a 'track killer', had earned him the reputation of being a fearless driver.

Then he returned to Europe, to the court of King Frank, who had high hopes of overcoming the likely problems of the '99 Williams thanks to two fast and impetuous drivers such as Alex Zanardi and Ralf Schumacher.

Instead, 1999 got off to a disappointing start for the Italian driver. In the ten races before the German GP, he retired eight times and only twice, at Montecarlo (8th) and Silverstone (11th) did he manage to reach the chequered flag, but way down the field.

Alessandro Zanardi, born in Bologna (Italy) 33 years ago, made his F1 debut in 1991 with a Jordan at the Spanish GP, finishing 9th. Then, still in F1, he raced 25 times for Minardi and Lotus between 1991 and 1994, picking up one point.

In 1995 his big break came in the USA, with Chip Ganassi, when he finished third in the 1996 championship. In '97 and '98 he then won the championship with the same team and the same car (Reynard-Honda). Zanardi won a total of 15 races in the CART championship.

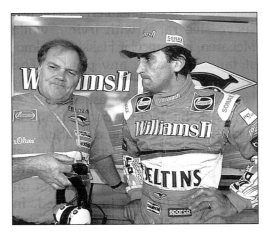

Monaco .. there's a GP out there somewhere!

The VIPs, the prices, the 'boat-show', the festivities and the beautiful women who revolve around F1 almost make up a Grand Prix within a Grand Prix at Montecarlo.

Or is it maybe the other way round?

On this particular occasion, the court of Prince Ranieri saw the arrival of world-famous footballers Gabriele Batistuta and Rui Costa, the cinematic Batman, Val Kilmer, as well as the usual names Briatore and Naomi Campbell.

As always, the Montecarlo GP was graced with the presence of Gianni Agnelli, Sarah Ferguson and the King of Sweden, who had just come from a private trip to Maranello.

There was a fantastic 'boat show' in the harbour, where mooring fees were the trifling sum of $10,000 for three days.

Amongst the boats was 'Anaconda', the latest acquisition of Eddie Irvine.

For four days, the peaceful town of Montecarlo is transformed into a 'theatre of the absurd'. The signs outside the restaurants along the circuit, normally with a fixed menu at $15, suddenly sprout an extra nought and the Hotel de Paris has a mile-long waiting-list for a place at a table on the famous terrace, where the 'lunch plus GP' package costs $700.

In the photo - sequence: the Duke of Kent with J. Stewart, Briatore and Naomi, Melinda Messenger, Val Kilmer, Sarah Ferguson and Mansuur Ojen.

Hakkinen and misfortune

At the mid-point of the season, despite Schumacher's retirement due to his incident at Silverstone, Ferrari won two successive races with Irvine, while McLaren, in particular Hakkinen, almost failed to score any points. The performance of Ferrari and Irvine was fantastic but to be honest, it must be said that the 1998 World Champion could not have been more unlucky.

At Silverstone, Hakkinen lost a wheel on lap 20. In Austria, team-mate Coulthard made contact with him on lap 1 while he was in the lead. In Germany on lap 26, when he was cha-

sing after the two Ferraris, a rear tyre exploded before the curve marking entry into the Motodrom. His McLaren pirouetted four times and ended up in the tyre wall. In a way, he was lucky that no other driver was around and that the pirouettes slowed his McLaren down considerably before the impact. Before the incident however, Mika had had another problem during the pit-stop, which cost him the lead. The nozzle on the refuelling rig refused to engage properly and the mechanics had to use Coulthard's rig. The stop lasted over 23 seconds. An eternity.

Mika Salo arrives ...

At 15.20 Italian time on 13 July 1999, Ferrari issued a press release saying that Mika Salo had been signed for the next rounds of the championship until Michael Schumacher returned.

Mika Salo is 33 years of age, was born in Helsinki (Finland) and lives in London.

That was a busy July week for Mika Salo. On Monday he was called by Ferrari, on Tuesday he signed the contract and ... on Saturday he got married to Noriko Ende, a young Japanese model who has been his girlfriend for years.

Mika Salo made his debut in F1 in 1994 for Lotus in the Japanese GP, finishing 10th.

In his career, he raced for Lotus in 1994 (2 Grand Prixs), from '95 to '97 with Tyrrell (50 GPs), in 1998 with Arrows (2 races) and in '99 with BAR in 3 Grand Prixs, in place of the Brazilian Riccardo Zonta, who was injured in his home race.

His best result was 4th in the Monaco GP in 1998.

Considered to be a nice guy by the entire F1 Circus, Mika is a close friend of Jacques Villeneuve, with whom he often spends holidays together in Finland. He arrived in F1 with a reputation for being a fast, aggressive driver but the cars he has driven have rarely helped him to demonstrate his full ability.

"This is the greatest opportunity of my life" he said in the short press conference at Maranello immediately after the signing of the accord and shortly before stepping into his Ferrari for a quick test around Fiorano.

It's true: it is a great opportunity but also a great responsibility for at least three reasons.

The first is that the eyes of the world will be on him. Is he as fast as he is made out to be? We will see.

The second is that inevitably comparisons will be made with Irvine and, at a distance, with Schumacher, starting with the Austrian GP.

The third is that Ferrari are still in the running for the Drivers' (with Irvine) and above all the Constructors' championship. Will Mika be able to earn the points for Ferrari?.

Mika Salo's first time

One week's testing on Ferrari's private test track at Fiorano, then his wedding in Helsinki and immediately after, the race in Austria.

It was not easy for Mika to get used to such a sophisticated car as the F399, more powerful and sensitive than anything he had driven previously.

Furthermore in such a short period of time he only had the chance to get to know the car without being able to modify the settings to suit his driving style. Mika had to 'trust' the suggestions of the engineers and Eddie Irvine before taking cautiously to the track.

On Friday during free practice in Austria, it was rather disconcerting to see the number 3 Ferrari bringing up the rear, especially after an 'off' had allowed him to do only a few laps.

On Saturday, with 7th place on the starting-grid, six-tenths away from team-mate Eddie and one-and-a-half seconds off pole position, Salo had recovered some of his optimism.

In the race, after a good start, Salo was fifth at the first corner but contact with Herbert forced him into the pits to change his damaged nose-cone, dropping him down the field. An overall ninth position demonstrated only that Salo had a quiet race, without taking any risks and keeping at bay his instinctive attacking qualities.

It was all good practice for the German GP which is held one week later, especially as Mika cannot carry out any more private tests due to the introduction of new norms.

Eddie the irrepressible braggart

After the incident to Schummy at Silverstone and before arriving in Austria, Eddie Irvine had amazed journalists (and also Ferrari bosses) with declarations such as ".... I'm on course for the world championship .... I'm going to win in Austria ...", almost as if Hakkinen and Coulthard were just two normal adversaries, easy to beat.

On Saturday, after official qualifying, he calmly commented on his third place on the grid, one second down on the McLarens, almost as if he hadn't bothered going any faster ... to avoid starting on the dirtier side of the track.

When after the race he stepped down off the top of the podium and was surrounded by journalists from all over the world, he looked at them with a sly, ironic smile, as if to say "What are you looking at me like that for? When I don't have to do my job as second driver, I go out to win, that's all".

Eddie might not be the best driver on the track, but he is certainly one of the nicest and most easy-going guys around.

He also has a great quality: he manages to give back a bit of humanity to the aseptic world of F1. In interviews, he alternates serious replies about technical matters with comments such as "the smoke coming out of my Ferrari at the end of the race? No, that was smoke coming out of my head because I had to concentrate on keeping Coulthard behind me".

All you have to do is look at the anxious face of Ferrari's Stefania Bocchi, who is like a shadow to the drivers, during the post-race interviews. It seems that at any moment she feared some sort of embarrassing comment about the absent Schumacher. Instead Irvine could only sympathise with Schumacher "Now I understand how Michael feels about being under pressure from the press and Ferrari fans" as well as "You journalists are so stressful, that's enough, I'm going to bed".

Well done Eddie, but things start getting difficult from here on. If you can't repeat your Austrian win, everyone will say it was a fluke. But if, with a bit of luck, like in Austria, you can continue fighting for the title, then Ferrari will have regained some of the sympathy and warmth it had lost with Schumacher.

Alain Prost's difficult moment

Four-times F1 world champion ('85, '86, '89 and '93) Alain Prost could never have imagined he was going to face such major difficulties as team manager when he took over Team Ligier in 1997, changing its name to Prost the following year.

The original idea was to prevent the last-remaining French F1 team from vanishing and to give life to a new all-French team run by the greatest driver France has ever had in F1: Alain Prost.

The tradition and experience of Ligier combined with the might of Peugeot was expected to produce some good results from 1998 onwards.

This would have catalysed the attention of the major French sponsors and the enthusiasm of the public around Team Prost.

Instead 1998 ended with just one point in the Manufacturers' standings, and the Prost team was even outclassed by Sauber, Arrows and Stewart.

The lack of results produced all sorts of problems, accusations and counter-accusations.

1998 might have ended badly, but 1999 was hardly much better as the Prost team had scored just two points by mid-season: sixth places for Panis in Brazil and for Trulli in Spain.

Not much to warm the hearts of the sponsors, almost all French, and to convince them to renew their backing for the following season.

But the most worrying aspect for Alain Prost is the rapport with Peugeot, where not everyone is in favour of continuing the manufacturer's involvement in F1.

It is true that Peugeot are contractually tied to Prost until the year 2000, but it is one thing to have an enthusiastic partner alongside and another to have one that is only there to avoid paying a hefty penalty for non-fulfilment of contract.

Furthermore, should Peugeot abandon the team, even after the contract expires, that would be the end of Alain Prost's dream of creating an all-French team, one in which his partners are also share-holders.

The driver of the future

This is probably the first time ever that so much has been said in Formula 1 about a driver ... who has yet to race.

The driver in question is Nick Heidfeld, a 22 year-old German from Moenchengladbach, who easily won the 1999 International Formula 3000 Championship.

Heidfeld is to all intents and purposes a Mercedes driver, after the Stuttgart manufacturer put him under contract in 1996. It is thanks to the support of Mercedes that in just three years Nick has managed to accumulate a formidable amount of experience for such a young driver.

He has been McLaren-Mercedes test-driver for the past three years and has already notched up more miles driving a F1 car than most current F1 drivers.

In F3000 he took part in the 1998 championship, winning three rounds (Montecarlo, Hockenheim and Budapest) and finishing second overall behind Juan-Pablo Montoya.

As mentioned before, Nick Heidfeld easily won the 1999 championship, winning four rounds out of ten and clinching the title at the eighth round.

His driver curriculum also includes the 1994 German Formula Ford 1600 title, with 8 wins out of 9 races, and the 1995 International Formula Ford 1800 Championship.

In 1999 Heidfeld took part in the Le Mans 24 Hours race alongside Peter Dumbreck in the Mercedes which when the latter was driving was involved in a spectacular incident, luckily without any consequences for the driver.

Millions of TV viewers watched as the silver Mercedes CLR literally took off on the Mulsanne Straight and cartwheeled into the woods on the side of the most famous track in the world.

Formula 1 is on the horizon for the young German driver. Mercedes might give him to Jordan 'on loan' for the 2000 season so that he picks up some experience away from the spotlights of Team McLaren, or to Prost which gave him a test-drive in 1999 at Silverstone.

It all seems a little bit similar to the career of a certain Michael Schumacher who in 1991 began his rise to the top of F1 in a Jordan.

And the similarities don't end there ....

Nick also began in karting, coincidentally on the same Kerpen track as Schumacher, and like Schummy he too has a younger brother who races in F3 ...

The circuit of the year 2000

On Friday 15th October, Formula 1 engines were officially fired up for the first time at the spectacular Sepang circuit in Malaysia.

Construction work began in November 1997 and the circuit was inaugurated on 9th March 1999 (14 months later !). The circuit is at the centre of an complex that also includes an amusement park, a go-kart track and international-standard hotels, while Kuala Lumpur International Airport is just 10 minutes away.

But the extraordinary thing about the circuit is the buildings, which, due to the fact that they were built up from scratch, are the most modern, elegant and technologically avant-guard ever seen. In addition, each building inside the circuit stands out for sheer size and luxury. The 30 pit garages, equipped with air conditioning and every type of power supply, each have a surface area of 200 sq m (24 m x 8 m) and contain office space and even a small kitchen.

The press centre has a total of 400 workspaces for media, all fitted with computer terminals and fibre-optic cable connections, as well as monitors and closed-circuit television, which with 27 fixed positions can cover the entire track.

Teams and sponsors have suites available for VIP guests. Everything is housed in outstandingly spectacular structures, highlighted by the symbol of the circuit, Canopy Tower.

The track has a width that ranges from 16 to 22 metres and measures a total of 5.542 kms, with 14 curves, including 5 which are long and very fast, and two which are almost hairpins, to be taken at sub-100 kph speed. Below a photograph of the circuit and the track with Canopy Tower in the background.

Canopy Tower

Jean Alesi at the court of Alain Prost

Jean Alesi is without a shadow of doubt one of the nicest and most affable drivers around in modern-day Formula 1. He appears to have remained eternally youthful, with a smile on his face that made him an idol of the crowd, especially the Italian tifosi, when he drove for Ferrari. At 37 years of age however, the French driver is a now man fulfilled, a good father and fixed companion to Kumiko, his partner for the last few years. Despite having competed in 167 Grand Prixs (winning only one - Canada '95 with Ferrari), he still has the same enthusiasm and desire to win as he had at the start of his career.

It was with this desire to win and this smile that he appeared before journalists on 24th August to confirm that he had signed for two years with the team run by Alain Prost, his friend and 1991 Ferrari team-mate. Two years and 10 million dollars to take the all-French F1 team onto the podium.

A change in the regulations?

They have been talking about it for a year or so, but now it seems that the time has come to make a decision.

For some time now, the drivers have been complaining about the use of grooved tyres, which in their opinion are dangerous and do not reduce speed at all.

These constant complaints have led Bernie Ecclestone to have a closer look at all aspects of 'his world'.

His aims are clearly more safety but also more exciting races.

The drivers are asking for greater attention to be paid to safety and many of them, in particular those from smaller teams, are asking to be able to compete with the larger teams on a competitive level.

To do this, there must be a reduction in excessive sophisticated development, which is only possible in the top teams. What can be done about it?

Eliminate carbon-fibre brakes to benefit the braver drivers?

Go back to slick tyres?

Standardise spoilers and aerodynamic devices?

Ecclestone listens to everyone, accepts suggestions and meditates on his next moves.

Also because to the problems of the drivers and the teams he must add his own, which are to make the 'show' more interesting and exciting.

He is the man who owns the television rights and as a result F1's impact on TV viewers around the world.

More spectators and more viewers mean more sponsors.

This is not a problem to be ignored, especially in view of a progressive withdrawal of the cigarette companies.

Ecclestone is convinced that F1 is attractive to other types of sponsors even without the tobacco companies and if he is convinced of this, it probably means there are already a number of sponsors knocking at the door, but he also knows that replacing a tried-and-tested product is not such an easy thing to do.

The main thing is to increase audiences, in order to encourage new investment.

A first solution could be to extend the duration of the Grand Prix weekend by having official qualifying on Friday, as it was before, and to make it more competitive by making the average times of the two days' qualifying sessions valid for the starting-grid.

A brief look at Formula 1 regulations

The cars

• Wings, which must be fixed (a controversial point at the start of the '99 championship: were they really fixed?) must be a maximum of 140 cms wide at the front, 100 cms at the rear, and positioned a maximum of 100 cms from the ground.

• Brakes must be fitted with a twin circuit. They can have a maximum thickness of 2.8 cms and a diameter of 27.8 cms.

• 1999 tyres must have four grooves and a maximum diameter of 66 cms.

• Front wheels must be no wider than 25.5 cms, and the rear wheels no wider than 38 cms.

100 cm.

100 cm.

140 cm.

• There is no actual limit to the length of a single-seater F1 car, but maximum width is 180 cms. Minimum weight including the driver must be 600 kgs. Here is a list of '99 drivers with their weight (in Kgs) and height (in Cms).

Driver	Weight	Height
A. Wurz	82.5	186
R. Schumacher	79.0	178
D. Coulthard	77.0	182
E. Irvine	77.0	178
O. Panis	77.0	173
M. Schumacher	76.5	174
R. Barrichello	76.5	172
A. Zanardi	75.5	176
P. De La Rosa	74.0	178
J. Alesi	73.5	170
M. Hakkinen	73.5	179
P. Diniz	71.5	178
M. Gené	71.5	173
G. Fisichella	70.5	172
D. Hill	70.0	182
H.H. Frentzen	68.5	178
J. Villeneuve	67.5	168
T. Takagi	66.5	180
J. Herbert	65.5	167
M. Salo	65.0	175
R. Zonta	64.0	172
J. Trulli	63.5	173
L. Badoer	59.5	171

• The engine, with a maximum displacement of 3000 cc, can have up to 12 cylinders, even though all the '99 engines have 10 cylinders. Rotary engines are not allowed.

Qualifying and Race

• During a GP weekend (qualifying and race), each car has 8 sets of dry-weather tyres available.

• The maximum number of cars in the race is 24, even though 22 cars from 11 teams make up the 1999 grid.

• Drivers who do not set a time that is 7% slower than pole position do not qualify for the race.
A controversial exception was made, in the French GP, when due to bad weather conditions, 5 drivers (Hill, Takagi, De La Rosa, Gené and Badoer) were officially outside the 107% qualifying time at the end of the session.

• The most important flags waved by marshalls along the race-track are: BLUE (to warn a driver he is about to be overtaken or that he must let himself be overtaken), YELLOW (general danger on the track, no overtaking), YELLOW/RED STRIPES (oil on track or slippery surface), WHITE (ambulance on track), RED (race stopped), BLACK with number of car (competitor must stop) and GREEN (end of danger).

• Limitations on testing have been introduced in 1999. During the championship, teams have a total of 50 test days available. Half of these are on circuits and on dates established by the Constructors Federation and the other half at the choice of teams as long as they are on authorized circuits.

Cars lose pieces!

Melbourne (Australia) - Away they go again … just four months after the final race of '98 in Japan. Months dedicated to the design of new cars, to the search for increasingly extreme technical and aerodynamic solutions and the problems, as always, are highlighted in the first few races.

In Australia the main problem was wings, which were more fragile than in the past because they were more elastic and therefore more susceptible to high speeds.

Villeneuve found this out at his own expense with a high-speed spin which pitched him into the wall.

The same thing had already happened to Herbert with the Stewart at the Barcelona test session, to Wurz with the Benetton and Trulli with the Prost. That these were not isolated incidents was demonstrated by the fact that in Australia the cars were losing pieces all over the place.

Schummy found himself with a damaged front wing, while his younger brother, not to be outdone, left a 'barge board' on the track.

There was even a protest (from Damon Hill) for the excessive risks, while someone else complained that the extreme solutions invented by the top teams might be applied in a more makeshift, and therefore more dangerous, way by the smaller teams.

At the start of '99, the FIA said it would keep an eye on things and intervene in case the problem should occur again. After Melbourne, it didn't.

Too much… electronics

Before it was the engine or the tyres that were the biggest problems for racing-cars. Engine failures or punctures were the unknown factors in every GP.

As the year 2000 approaches, there is one component in F1 that appears to have become decisive: the steering wheel. For the past two or three seasons we have seen it become a real concentration of technology, but that it was so delicate was only discovered in 1999.

At Melbourne Schumacher had to come into the pits because his steering wheel no longer responded as it should. Strange? Not at all! The same thing happened to his 'steering wheel-gearshift' unit in France. Television spectators around the world saw a Ferrari engineer rush into the pit lane holding a brand-new steering wheel for Schummy and change it in a few seconds. An object just a few centimetres in diameter which contains numerous buttons, lights and led display indicating the engine revs. With the steering wheel the driver can change gear, speak with the pits, have a drink, open the fuel filler cap, receive messages and adjust the air-fuel intake. A few grams of carbon-fibre costing well over 20,000 dollars.

Pages 50-51
Poor Jacques! The Canadian
knew it wasn't going to be an easy year
with a totally new car, but little did
he know that he would almost never
see the chequered flag ...

Pages 49
Frentzen's yellow Jordan
flashes past a background
of blue Montecarlo sea.
It was a fantastic season
for the German driver,
who was fourth in Monaco
and almost always in the
points in the other races.

Pages 52-53
Niki Lauda,
winner of 3 world titles
between '75 and '85,
having a chat with
Ralf Schumacher.
The 24 year-old German
matured a lot in 1999
even with a Williams
that was not as
competitive as expected.

Pages 54-55
From
'stand-in'
for injured
colleagues
to star with
Ferrari and
favourite
of the Italian
tifosi in just
five races:
that's

Mika Salo, here with his wife Noriko
at Monza, before the race that saw
him step onto the podium for
the second time in his career.

Pages 56-57
A funny-looking
Eddie Irvine surrounded
by beautiful women in
the paddock; after Ferrari,
his other great passion in life.

Pages 58-59
Pit stop for the
Williams of Ralf
Schumacher,
who had an
aggressive race
at Monza where
he finished
second behind
Frentzen. On the
Italian circuit,
the two Williams
finally put together an encouraging
performance for the future.

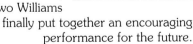

Pages 60-61
The two great rivals,
Schummy and Mika,
at the Monaco circuit,
where they finished
first and third
respectively.

Pages 62-63
H.H. Frentzen had never
before been such a major
protagonist in the championship.
The 32 year-old from
Moenchengladbach, Germany
found the climate of tranquillity he
was looking for in team Jordan.

Pages 64-65
Maxi-screen
for Schumacher,
convalescing at home
after his crash
at Silverstone
and interviewed live
for the joy of Italian tifosi
before the start of the
Hungarian GP.

Pages 66-67
All things considered,
McLaren's year was
a difficult one to decipher.
The car was clearly
the best around but there
were so many mistakes ...
and so much bad luck!

Pages 68-69
The 28 year-old
Scottish driver,
Coulthard, in Spain
during a test session
at the start of the
season. David was in
his fourth year with
McLaren and has
already renewed his
contract for 2000.

Pages 70-71
After two days qualifying,
team meetings,
sponsor commitments
and interviews ...
the culminating moment
of the GP weekend
comes when the cars
line up on the grid.

Pages 72-73
One driver who failed
to live up to expectations
in '99 was Alexander Wurz,
the 25 year-old Austrian
who drove for Benetton.
The only record
he continues to hold
is that of being the tallest
driver (1.86m) in the circus.

Pages 74-75
This year's championship
was full of confusion
due to numerous strange
events and incidents.
Inexplicable spins
and retirements,
fragile roll-bars,
wheels that fell
off after pit-stops ...

Pages 76-77
Formula 1 is not only a spectacle
out on the track. Today the paddock
is a luxurious meeting-place for VIPs from all
over the world. Just look at the Benetton,
BAR and Ferrari motorhomes,
as well as the exclusive Paddock Club.

PAG. 80
Mika Hakkinen, 31 years
old from Vantaa (Finland),
128 GPs and the 1998
World Championship to his name.
After Schumacher's crash,
it all seemed so easy for Hakkinen
in 1999, but ...

Pages 78-79
Ralf Schumacher can no longer
be considered 'Michael's younger
brother'. In 1999 he produced some
fantastic performances and scored a
good number of points for the Drivers'
championship, despite not having
a competitive car.

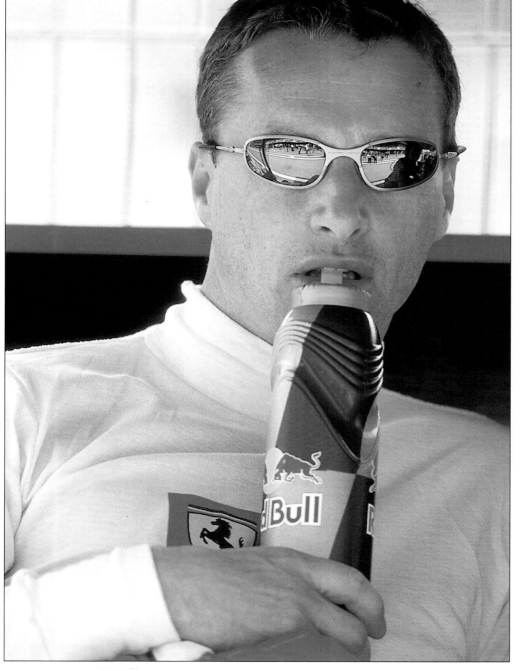

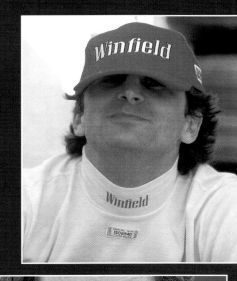

1949 1950

F1

1999

Year	World Championship positions	Events in Motorsport	Events in the World
50	1 **Farina** (I) (Alfa Romeo) 2 **Fangio** (RA) (Alfa Romeo) 3 **Fagioli** (I) (Alfa Romeo) -	The World Drivers' Championship was officially born. The first champion was Italian Giuseppe Farina in a 1500cc Alfa Romeo 158. Winning three Grand Prixs (Britain, Switzerland and Italy), Farina finished ahead of his team-mates J.M. Fangio and Fagioli.	
51	1 **Fangio** (RA) (Alfa Romeo) 2 **Ascari** (I) (Ferrari) 3 **Gonzalez** (RA) (Ferrari) -	• For the first time ever, disc brakes are fitted to a racing car, at the Indianapolis 500 race. • In Formula 1 the Argentine ace J.M. Fangio wins the championship ahead of the Ferraris of Ascari and Gonzalez. ►	
52	1 **Ascari** (I) (Ferrari) 2 **Farina** (I) (Ferrari) 3 **Taruffi** (I) (Ferrari)	The front row of the Italian GP at Monza is made up of the three Ferraris of Ascari, Villoresi and Farina.	Dwight D. Eisenhower became President of the United States of America on 5th November.
53	1 **Ascari** (I) (Ferrari) 2 **Fangio** (RA) (Maserati) 3 **Farina** (I) (Ferrari) -	Tazio Nuvolari ► died on 1st August. He was buried with his helmet and traditional racing gear: yellow shirt and blue trousers.	Sir Edmund Hillary reached the peak of Mount Everest (8848 metres) together with the Nepalese Sherpa Tenzing.
54	1 **Fangio** (RA) (Maserati e Mercedes) 2 **Gonzalez** (RA) (Ferrari) 3 **Hawthorn** (GB) (Ferrari) -	Stirling Moss won his first F1 race on 29th May at Aintree.	Italian climbers Achille Compagnoni and Lino Lacedelli reached the top of K2, 8819 metres above sea level, the second-highest mountain in the world.
55	1 **Fangio** (RA) (Mercedes) 2 **Moss** (GB) (Mercedes) 3 **Castellotti** (I) (Lancia and Ferrari) -	• On 26th May, Alberto Ascari was killed at Monza. The twice World F1 Champion with the Ferrari 500-F2 in 1952 and 1953 was the son of Antonio Ascari. • The most tragic motor sport incident ever occurred on 12th June at Le Mans. Two drivers, Levegh (Mercedes) and Macklin (Austin Healey) collided and flew off the track into the crowd. Levegh and 81 spectators were killed. ►	
56	1 **Fangio** (RA) (Ferrari) 2 **Moss** (GB) (Maserati) 3 **Collins** (GB) (Ferrari) -	With Mercedes pulling out of the sport, the two great drivers of the time are signed by the two rival Italian manufacturer teams. Fangio goes to Ferrari (►) and Moss to Maserati.	

57	1 **Fangio** (RA) (Maserati) 2 **Moss** (GB) (Vanwall) 3 **Musso** (I) (Ferrari) -	• "Gentlemen, start your engines", the famous phrase at the start of the Indianapolis 500 race, was used for the first time. • Stirling Moss was the first British driver to win the British GP in a British car (Vanwall). ►	
58	1 **Hawthorn** (GB) (Ferrari) 2 **Moss** (GB) (Vanwall and Cooper-Climax) 3 **Brooks** (GB) (Vanwall) **Vanwall**	"Cosworth Engineering", a company specialized in the tuning of Ford engines, was created. Its two partners were Mike Costin and Keith Duckworth. The first Cosworth engine was fitted to a Lotus 49 in 1967.	
59	1 **Brabham** (AUS) (Cooper-Climax) 2 **Brooks** (GB) (Ferrari) 3 **Moss** (GB) (Cooper-Climax and BRM) **Cooper**	Mike Hawthorn, who won the 1958 F1 championship, was killed in a car crash near Guildford, Surrey (England).	In January, a revolutionary movement led by Fidel Castro overthrew the Batista dictatorship.
60	1 **Brabham** (AUS) (Cooper-Climax) 2 **McLaren** (NZ) (Cooper-Climax) 3 **Moss** (GB) (Lotus-Climax and Cooper-Climax) **Cooper**	• Lotus won its first Grand Prix. Stirling Moss took the car to victory at Montecarlo. • Colin Chapman discovered a young, virtually unknown driver. His name was Jim Clark and he was born in Scotland in 1936. • Ferrari built its first rear-engine car - the 256P.	Democrat J.F. Kennedy defeated Republican candidate Nixon to become the President of the United States.
61	1 **P. Hill** (USA) (Ferrari) 2 **Von Trips** (D) (Ferrari) 3 **Moss** (GB) (Lotus-Climax) **Ferrari**	In the French GP, Giancarlo Baghetti, driving a Ferrari, became the first man to win in his first F1 Grand Prix.	• On 12th April, Soviet cosmonaut Yuri Gagarin became the first man to travel in space on board the satellite Vostok 1. • The Communist East German government constructed the Berlin Wall in August to divide the city into two parts.
62	1 **G. Hill** (GB) (BRM) 2 **Clark** (GB) (Lotus-Climax) 3 **McLaren** (NZ) (Cooper-Climax) **BRM**	Jim Clark won his first F1 GP in Belgium in a Lotus. The following year, he went on to win the World Championship and Lotus the Constructors' title.	
63	1 **Clark** (GB) (Lotus-Climax) 2 **G. Hill** (GB) (BRM) 3 **Ginther** (USA) (BRM) **Lotus**	• Jack Brabham, in a Brabham-Climax, won a non-championship F1 race in Stuttgart. It was the first time that a driver had won in a car of his own construction. • Ken Tyrrell created the team of the same name. The driver in Formula 3 was a young Scot: Jackie Stewart.	On 22nd November in Dallas, Kennedy was assassinated in circumstances which still today remain unclear; Vice-President L.B. Johnson took over as President.

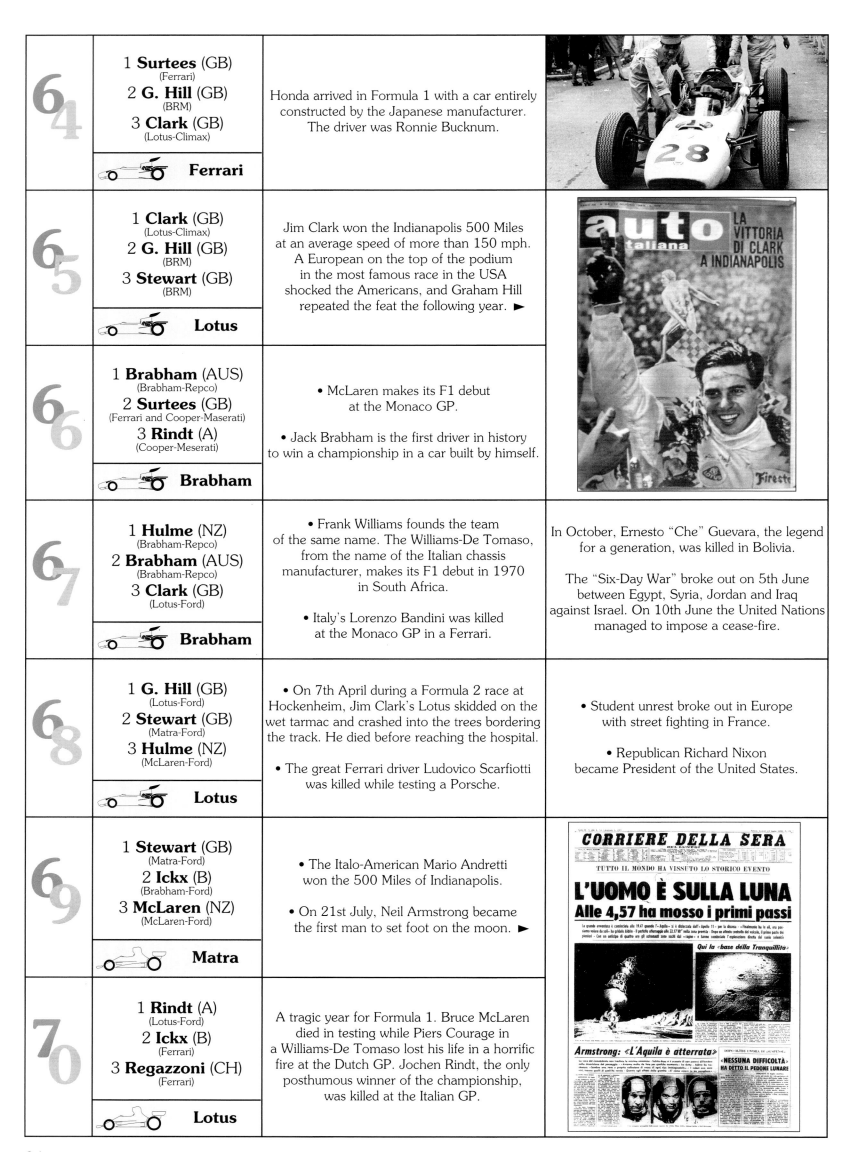

64	1 **Surtees** (GB) (Ferrari) 2 **G. Hill** (GB) (BRM) 3 **Clark** (GB) (Lotus-Climax) **Ferrari**	Honda arrived in Formula 1 with a car entirely constructed by the Japanese manufacturer. The driver was Ronnie Bucknum.
65	1 **Clark** (GB) (Lotus-Climax) 2 **G. Hill** (GB) (BRM) 3 **Stewart** (GB) (BRM) **Lotus**	Jim Clark won the Indianapolis 500 Miles at an average speed of more than 150 mph. A European on the top of the podium in the most famous race in the USA shocked the Americans, and Graham Hill repeated the feat the following year. ▶
66	1 **Brabham** (AUS) (Brabham-Repco) 2 **Surtees** (GB) (Ferrari and Cooper-Maserati) 3 **Rindt** (A) (Cooper-Meserati) **Brabham**	• McLaren makes its F1 debut at the Monaco GP. • Jack Brabham is the first driver in history to win a championship in a car built by himself.
67	1 **Hulme** (NZ) (Brabham-Repco) 2 **Brabham** (AUS) (Brabham-Repco) 3 **Clark** (GB) (Lotus-Ford) **Brabham**	• Frank Williams founds the team of the same name. The Williams-De Tomaso, from the name of the Italian chassis manufacturer, makes its F1 debut in 1970 in South Africa. • Italy's Lorenzo Bandini was killed at the Monaco GP in a Ferrari.
68	1 **G. Hill** (GB) (Lotus-Ford) 2 **Stewart** (GB) (Matra-Ford) 3 **Hulme** (NZ) (McLaren-Ford) **Lotus**	• On 7th April during a Formula 2 race at Hockenheim, Jim Clark's Lotus skidded on the wet tarmac and crashed into the trees bordering the track. He died before reaching the hospital. • The great Ferrari driver Ludovico Scarfiotti was killed while testing a Porsche.
69	1 **Stewart** (GB) (Matra-Ford) 2 **Ickx** (B) (Brabham-Ford) 3 **McLaren** (NZ) (McLaren-Ford) **Matra**	• The Italo-American Mario Andretti won the 500 Miles of Indianapolis. • On 21st July, Neil Armstrong became the first man to set foot on the moon. ▶
70	1 **Rindt** (A) (Lotus-Ford) 2 **Ickx** (B) (Ferrari) 3 **Regazzoni** (CH) (Ferrari) **Lotus**	A tragic year for Formula 1. Bruce McLaren died in testing while Piers Courage in a Williams-De Tomaso lost his life in a horrific fire at the Dutch GP. Jochen Rindt, the only posthumous winner of the championship, was killed at the Italian GP.

67: In October, Ernesto "Che" Guevara, the legend for a generation, was killed in Bolivia.

The "Six-Day War" broke out on 5th June between Egypt, Syria, Jordan and Iraq against Israel. On 10th June the United Nations managed to impose a cease-fire.

68: • Student unrest broke out in Europe with street fighting in France.

• Republican Richard Nixon became President of the United States.

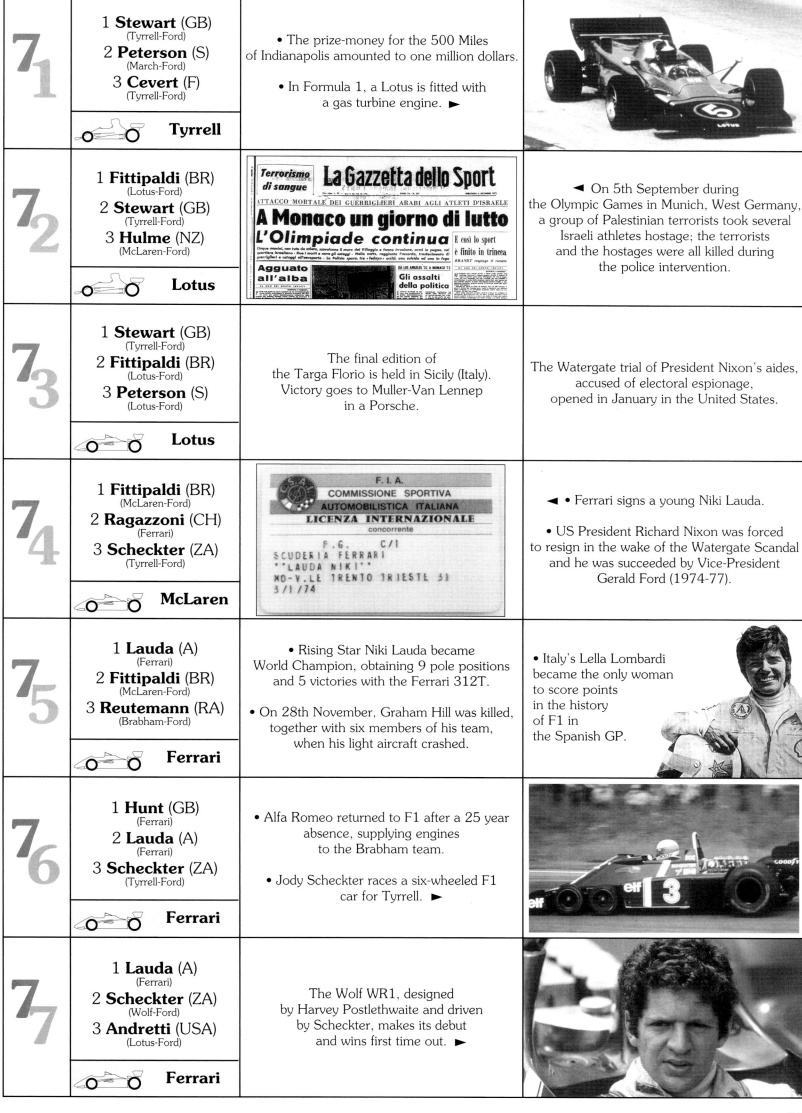

71	1 **Stewart** (GB) (Tyrrell-Ford) 2 **Peterson** (S) (March-Ford) 3 **Cevert** (F) (Tyrrell-Ford) **Tyrrell**	• The prize-money for the 500 Miles of Indianapolis amounted to one million dollars. • In Formula 1, a Lotus is fitted with a gas turbine engine. ►	
72	1 **Fittipaldi** (BR) (Lotus-Ford) 2 **Stewart** (GB) (Tyrrell-Ford) 3 **Hulme** (NZ) (McLaren-Ford) **Lotus**	*Terrorismo di sangue* **La Gazzetta dello Sport** ATTACCO MORTALE DEI GUERRIGLIERI ARABI AGLI ATLETI D'ISRAELE **A Monaco un giorno di lutto** **L'Olimpiade continua**	◄ On 5th September during the Olympic Games in Munich, West Germany, a group of Palestinian terrorists took several Israeli athletes hostage; the terrorists and the hostages were all killed during the police intervention.
73	1 **Stewart** (GB) (Tyrrell-Ford) 2 **Fittipaldi** (BR) (Lotus-Ford) 3 **Peterson** (S) (Lotus-Ford) **Lotus**	The final edition of the Targa Florio is held in Sicily (Italy). Victory goes to Muller-Van Lennep in a Porsche.	The Watergate trial of President Nixon's aides, accused of electoral espionage, opened in January in the United States.
74	1 **Fittipaldi** (BR) (McLaren-Ford) 2 **Ragazzoni** (CH) (Ferrari) 3 **Scheckter** (ZA) (Tyrrell-Ford) **McLaren**	F.I.A. COMMISSIONE SPORTIVA AUTOMOBILISTICA ITALIANA **LICENZA INTERNAZIONALE** concorrente P.G. C/1 SCUDERIA FERRARI ''LAUDA NIKI'' MO-V.LE TRENTO TRIESTE 31 3/1/74	◄ • Ferrari signs a young Niki Lauda. • US President Richard Nixon was forced to resign in the wake of the Watergate Scandal and he was succeeded by Vice-President Gerald Ford (1974-77).
75	1 **Lauda** (A) (Ferrari) 2 **Fittipaldi** (BR) (McLaren-Ford) 3 **Reutemann** (RA) (Brabham-Ford) **Ferrari**	• Rising Star Niki Lauda became World Champion, obtaining 9 pole positions and 5 victories with the Ferrari 312T. • On 28th November, Graham Hill was killed, together with six members of his team, when his light aircraft crashed.	• Italy's Lella Lombardi became the only woman to score points in the history of F1 in the Spanish GP.
76	1 **Hunt** (GB) (Ferrari) 2 **Lauda** (A) (Ferrari) 3 **Scheckter** (ZA) (Tyrrell-Ford) **Ferrari**	• Alfa Romeo returned to F1 after a 25 year absence, supplying engines to the Brabham team. • Jody Scheckter races a six-wheeled F1 car for Tyrrell. ►	
77	1 **Lauda** (A) (Ferrari) 2 **Scheckter** (ZA) (Wolf-Ford) 3 **Andretti** (USA) (Lotus-Ford) **Ferrari**	The Wolf WR1, designed by Harvey Postlethwaite and driven by Scheckter, makes its debut and wins first time out. ►	

78	**1 Andretti** (USA) (Lotus-Ford) **2 Peterson** (S) (Lotus-Ford) **3 Reutemann** (RA) (Ferrari) **Lotus**	• The Arrows team makes its debut in the Brazilian GP. • At Monza, Swedish driver Ronnie Peterson is involved in a crash at the start. He remains trapped in his burning car and dies in hospital later.	On 16th October, after the brief papacy of John Paul I (August-September), Polish Archbishop Karol Wojtyla became Pope under the name of John Paul II.
79	**1 Scheckter** (ZA) (Ferrari) **2 G. Villeneuve** (CDN) (Ferrari) **3 Jones** (AUS) (Williams-Ford) **Ferrari**	• At Kyalami, Gilles Villeneuve won the South African GP with the new Ferrari 312 T4 designed by Mauro Forghieri. • Two great drivers of the seventies, Niki Lauda and James Hunt, both retired from motor racing.	Margaret Thatcher of the Conservative Party becomes British Prime Minister. She would be known throughout the world as the 'Iron Lady'.
80	**1 Jones** (AUS) (Williams-Ford) **2 Piquet** (BR) (Brabham-Ford) **3 Reutemann** (RA) (Williams-Ford) **Williams**	Alfa Romeo returns to F1 with an all-Italian, Chiti-designed car.	
81	**1 Piquet** (BR) (Brabham-Ford) **2 Reutemann** (RA) (Williams-Ford) **3 Jones** (AUS) (Williams-Ford) **Williams**	• The Spanish GP at Jarama on 21st June saw one of the most exciting Grand Prixs in the history of Formula 1. Villeneuve won from Laffite, Watson, Reutemann and De Angelis, all separated by one second at the flag.	• The first Space Shuttle is launched in April. The US space plane is capable of returning home after a mission and landing like an aeroplane. • Hosni Mubarak becomes president of Egypt in October after the assassination of Sadat in a plot by military rebels.
82	**1 Rosberg** (SF) (Williams-Ford) **2 Pironi** (F) (Ferrari) **3 Watson** (GB) (McLaren-Ford) **Ferrari**	• On 8th May, Gilles Villeneuve was killed during qualifying for the Belgian GP, when he crashed into the car driven by Jochen Mass. • Colin Chapman, one of F1's great innovators and owner of Lotus, died of a heart attack in mysterious circumstances on 16th December at the age of 51.	The Falklands War between Britain and Argentina lasted from April to June and ended with Argentina renouncing any claims to the islands.
83	**1 Piquet** (BR) (Brabham-BMW) **2 Prost** (F) (Renault) **3 Arnoux** (F) (Ferrari) **Ferrari**	The year of the turbo. Brazilian Nelson Piquet (Brabham-BMW) wins his second world title.	
84	**1 Lauda** (A) (McLaren-Porsche) **2 Prost** (F) (McLaren-Porsche) **3 De Angelis** (I) (Lotus-Renault) **McLaren**	The Benetton company enters F1 as sponsor of Alfa Romeo. It would become a team in its own right in 1986.	

85	1 **Prost** (F) (McLaren-Porsche) 2 **Alboreto** (I) (Ferrari) 3 **Rosberg** (SF) (Williams-Honda) **McLaren**	The Italian Minardi team makes its F1 debut in the Brazilian GP. ▶ Tyre manufacturers 'invent' qualifying tyres that last just 2 or 3 laps.	
86	1 **Prost** (F) (McLaren-Porsche) 2 **Mansell** (GB) (Williams-Honda) 3 **Piquet** (BR) (Williams-Honda) **Williams**	With the purchase of the Toleman outfit, the Benetton Group makes its entry into F1. This is the start of an adventure that would take the Benetton team to the Constructors' title in 1995 and the Drivers' title in '94 and '95 with Schumacher.	On 26th April, the Chernobyl nuclear power plant in the USSR malfunctioned and caused the world's worst reactor disaster to date. The toxic clouds reached Western Europe.
87	1 **Piquet** (BR) (Williams-Honda) 2 **Mansell** (GB) (Williams-Honda) 3 **Senna** (BR) (Lotus-Honda) **Williams**	Ayrton Senna scored Lotus' last victory in F1 at Detroit. Satoru Nakajima ▶ became the first Japanese F1 driver, sparking of a wave of interest in F1 in the country.	
88	1 **Senna** (BR) (McLaren-Honda) 2 **Prost** (F) (McLaren-Honda) 3 **Berger** (A) (Ferrari) **McLaren**	• Enzo Ferrari dies in Modena on 14th August. A few days later, at Monza, the Ferraris of Berger and Alboreto score a historic 1-2 at the Italian GP. • In Adelaide on 13th November, Alain Prost wins the Australian GP in a McLaren-Honda, the last Formula 1 race for 'turbo' cars.	
89	1 **Prost** (F) (McLaren-Honda) 2 **Senna** (BR) (McLaren-Honda) 3 **Patrese** (I) (Williams-Renault) **McLaren**	• Another Japanese colossus entered Formula 1 - Yamaha, supplying engines to the German Zakspeed team. • Jean Alesi, the French driver of Italian descent, made his F1 debut in the French GP for Tyrrell.	• Akihito became the new emperor of Japan after the death of Hirohito, while in Iran the Ayatollah Khomeini died in June. • In May, the Chinese military brutally put down a democratic protest in Tien An Men Square in Beijing, killing 7000 demonstrators.
90	1 **Senna** (BR) (McLaren-Honda) 2 **Prost** (F) (Ferrari) 3 **Piquet** (BR) (Benetton-Ford) **McLaren**	Prost and Senna, fighting for the championship, make (deliberate) contact at the first corner and go off the track. Senna wins the world championship.	• After the release from prison of the Black Leader Nelson Mandela, the South African government of De Klerk began the progressive abolition of the Apartheid regime. • The reunification of Germany was sanctioned on 3rd October and the Berlin Wall was pulled down on 9th November.
91	1 **Senna** (BR) (McLaren-Honda) 2 **Mansell** (GB) (Williams-Renault) 3 **Patrese** (I) (Williams-Renault) **McLaren**	• Jordan makes its F1 debut at the US Grand Prix in Phoenix. • The shortest race in F1 history - the Australian GP - is brought to an end by a thunderstorm after just 25 minutes. Senna was leading at the time. • One of the sport's leading figures, Jean-Marie Balestre, President of FISA, bows out of F1. He is replaced by Max Mosley, founder of March.	The Gulf War broke out in the night of 17th January: the UN attack on Iraq forced Saddam Hussein to surrender unconditionally and withdraw from Kuwait.

92	1 **Mansell** (GB) (Williams-Renault) 2 **Patrese** (I) (Williams-Renault) 3 **Schumacher** (D) (Benetton-Ford) **Williams**	• Ferrari celebrated its 500th GP in Hungary. • Michael Schumacher, driving a Benetton-Ford, won his first F1 GP at Spa, Belgium.	In February, the Maastricht Treaty, signed by EEC countries, was laying down the conditions for the process of European political and monetary integration, to be implemented by January 1999.
93	1 **Prost** (F) (Williams-Renault) 2 **Senna** (BR) (McLaren-Ford) 3 **D. Hill** (GB) (Williams-Renault) **Williams**	• Sauber makes its debut in the South African Grand Prix. • Ayrton Senna wins at Montecarlo for the fifth successive time. With his victory in 1987, Senna becomes the most successful driver ever at the Monaco GP. • On 15th August, Damon Hill takes his first F1 win at the Hungarian GP. ▶	
94	1 **Schumacher** (D) (Benetton-Ford) 2 **D. Hill** (GB) (Williams-Renault) 3 **Berger** (A) (Ferrari) **Williams**	The tragedy of Imola. Roland Ratzenberger (in qualifying) and Ayrton Senna (in the race) were both killed. The Brazilian champion went off the track on lap 5 and died in hospital four hours later.	On 6th May, Queen Elisabeth II and French President Francois Mitterand inaugurated the 50 km long Channel Tunnel. Construction work had started in 1987 and regular service began in August 1994.
95	1 **Schumacher** (D) (Benetton-Renault) 2 **D. Hill** (GB) (Williams-Renault) 3 **Coulthard** (GB) (Williams-Renault) **Benetton**	• A year of "firsts" in F1. J. Alesi (Ferrari) in Canada, ▶ J. Herbert (Benetton) in Britain and D. Coulthard (Williams) in Portugal all won their first Grand Prixs. • J. Villeneuve won the 500 Miles of Indianapolis and the Indy Car Championship, the youngest driver ever to do so. • J.M. Fangio died. He was born in Balcarce, Argentina in 1911. He was World Champion in 1951 (Alfa Romeo), in 1954 (Maserati and Mercedes), 1955 (Mercedes Benz), 1956 (Ferrari) and 1957 (Maserati).	
96	1 **D. Hill** (GB) (Williams-Renault) 2 **J. Villeneuve** (CDN) (Williams-Renault) 3 **Schumacher** (D) (Ferrari) **Williams**	• Damon Hill wins the World Drivers' Championship with Williams. This is the first time in F1 history that the son of a world champion (Graham Hill in 1962 and 1968) wins the title. • In his fourth F1 race, Jacques Villeneuve wins his first GP at the Nurburgring.	The centenary Olympic Games were held in Atlanta, USA. The decision to award the Games to the American city instead of Athens caused worldwide controversy.
97	1 **J. Villeneuve** (CDN) (Williams-Renault) 2 **Frentzen** (D) (Williams-Renault) 3 **Coulthard** (GB) (McLaren-Mercedes) **Williams**	• Team Stewart makes its F1 debut at the Australian GP. • Jacques Villeneuve, the son of the unforgettable Gilles, wins the F1 World Championship with Williams. ▶	
98	1 **Hakkinen** (SF) (McLaren-Mercedes) 2 **Schumacher** (D) (Ferrari) 3 **Coulthard** (GB) (McLaren-Mercedes) **McLaren**	Hakkinen is the second Finnish driver to win the F1 world championship. Keke Rosberg (currently his manager) was the first, winning the title in 1982 for Williams.	In America attention is focusing on the sex scandal involving Bill Clinton and Monica Lewinsky.

50 years of Evolution in Formula 1

An entire book would probably not be sufficient to relate 50 years of evolution in Formula 1. In the following pages, we have tried to document several curious or less well-known (but still important) aspects of this evolution.

Special thanks go to the companies that produce components, accessories and services for their information and photographs.

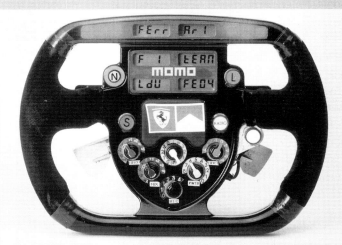

Hakkinen's crash helmet

From leather or even silk caps (a personal favourite of Achille Varzi) to iron helmets similar to those used in the war, to the latest-generation full-face helmet in lightweight material.

This is basically the evolution of a driver's most important safety component. But how are today's lightweight, resistant and even aerodynamic helmets built?

Today's helmets weigh slightly more than 1 kg and there is a reason for this. The lighter the helmet, the lesser the lateral force that is imposed on a driver's neck in fast curves, or in the case of impact against a crash-barrier in an incident.

ARAI, a company founded in Japan in 1937, supplies helmets to the world champion Mika Hakkinen as well as his team-mate Coulthard and other drivers such as Damon Hill and Rubens Barrichello. It uses a special fibre called ScLc, of military origin and this 'super' fibre has replaced glass-fibre.

Inside the helmet, a layer of variable-density polystyrene foam is fitted and the function of this is to 'absorb', in case of impact.

The outside of the helmet is made of an extremely hard material, ScLc, the function of which is to distribute the force of the impact all over the external surface and to prevent anything from penetrating the helmet.

Today the use of plastic materials allows helmets to be made with special shapes, creating small lateral 'stabilisers' that reduce turbulence, help internal ventilation or even channel the flow of air towards the air intakes of the engine behind the driver.

A helmet therefore also has an aerodynamic function.

But even for helmet accessories, research and development into the most advanced technologies is continuing.

Each component is made in fire-resistant material and even the ventilation or visor openings are designed in such a way as to make it almost impossible for flames to enter the helmet.

ARAI has even patented a double D-ring that acts as a lock for the kevlar straps and allows rapid release.

Another important component is the face visor, made of 3mm thick polycarbonate, with the possibility of attaching 'tear-off' strips.

Polycarbonate is a material that is highly resistant to scratches and knocks (at 300 kph even a fly becomes a blunt instrument!) and is extremely transparent.

Today's visors are also protected with a thin film that is capable of absorbing the humidity that forms inside the helmet (due to warmth and breathing) and prevents it from misting up during a GP.

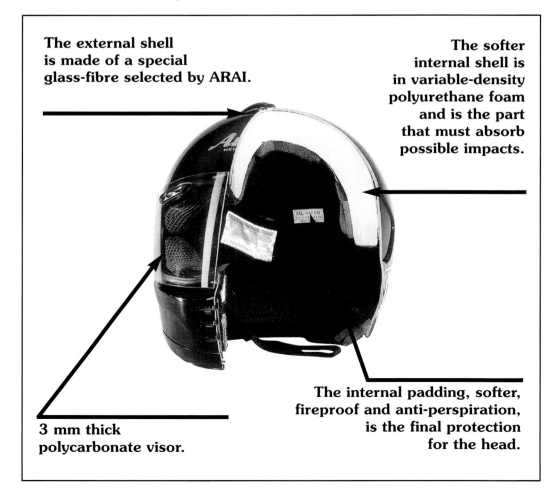

The external shell is made of a special glass-fibre selected by ARAI.

The softer internal shell is in variable-density polyurethane foam and is the part that must absorb possible impacts.

3 mm thick polycarbonate visor.

The internal padding, softer, fireproof and anti-perspiration, is the final protection for the head.

From steering wheels...to computer

Enzo Ferrari

Fifty years ago the steering wheel fitted to the first racing cars were made of wood usually with three or four metal spokes.

Then, with the increase in performance of racing cars, especially in corners, it was necessary to modify grip and change the steering wheel to satisfy the demands of individual drivers.

In 1964 John Surtees asked the Italian company, Momo, to create a steering wheel with two padded areas to improve grip. This solution was not exactly 'high-tech'; a bit of rubber and sticky tape were used to cover the wood.

Just for the record, Surtees and Ferrari won the Drivers' and Constructors' titles that year.

Some drivers also had a bright idea to improve grip: shortly before the start, they used to wet their gloves with drinking-water!

In 1982 René Arnoux made another suggestion to Momo to improve grip: reverse the leather (which some years back had replaced sticky tape as covering) so that the rough part was on the outside.

Today steering wheels are still covered with chamois leather but, since Arnoux's days, they have also sprouted numerous buttons on the spokes. The number of buttons has gradually increased so that today drivers are faced with a combination of steering wheel, instrument panel and computer.

Iron or aluminium spokes have been replaced with carbon-fibre and the simple nut that fixed the wheel to the steering column has been replaced by a quick-release ring.

Even the shape has changed, because cockpits have become much smaller or because each individual driver has asked to adapt them to his own personal style.

In 1995 Gerhard Berger asked Momo to produce a butterfly-shaped steering wheel with a double grip.

Jean Alesi, another Ferrari driver of

the early 1990s, preferred the classic 25 cm diameter steering wheel.

Even size underwent major changes!

A photograph of a young Enzo Ferrari, who raced in the 1920s, shows him driving a C.M.N. car with a steering wheel measuring almost 60 cm in diameter!

In the early 1950s, the first steering wheels in wood and iron had a diameter of 35 cm. The minimum dimension ever reached was the excessively small 24 cm steering wheel on the 1993 Jordan of Thierry Boutsen, before new regulations brought in wider cockpits and today's 27 cm diameter limit.

The steering wheel therefore might be just a few centimetres of lights and buttons for communicating with the pit lane or for regulating numerous functions ... but even a driver of the calibre of Mika Salo, on his debut in Ferrari, was heard to say that the biggest difficulty he had was not driving the car but getting to grips with the maze of buttons and lights he was confronted with.

1) Steering wheel and instrument panel of a 1970s March.

2) Cockpit of a 1968 Ferrari Dino.

3) Momo steering wheel for Gerhard Berger's 1994 Ferrari.

A curiosity: the limited-edition steering wheel (one!) produced by Momo for the Italian driver Alessandro Nannini with a shaped grip for his right hand which was severed (and then reattached) in a 1990 helicopter incident which ended his F1 career. After the incident, the President of Ferrari Luca di Montezemolo sent him best wishes for recovery and promised him that whenever he liked, he could drive a Ferrari F1. Montezemolo kept his promise two years after the incident and on 14th October 1992, Nannini drove a few laps in a F1 Ferrari on the Fiorano private test-track, using this steering wheel for the occasion.

Fuel devlopements over the years

In the 1950s, the cars driven by Ascari and Fangio used fuel that was similar to that normally available on the market.

In the 1970s, research by fuel companies involved in motorsport was almost entirely concentrated on the possibility of increasing the octane number and therefore the self-detonating power of fuels.

It was however in the 1980s, with the advent of turbo engines, that fuels became vitally important in the search for better performance. Turbocharger pressure and as a result, the need to increase engine resistance, increased in the continuing research that was characterised by massive numbers of engine failures in the races.

It was in that period that research began to develop, rather experimentally to say the least, when it was realised that at the end of a wet Grand Prix, the engines were in an excellent condition, without any signs of detonation on pistons and cylinder heads.

Thanks to this observation, engineers from AgipPetroli, Ferrari partner at the time, decided to adopt, successfully it must be added, a fuel injection system that mixed water with the fuel in the combustion chamber. This was called Emulsystem, and it had already been used in aeroplane engines during the Second World War.

The new F1 regulations introduced half-way through the 1980s, which limited fuel capacity and banned refuelling during the race, forced fuel companies, and therefore also Agip, to find other means of increasing performance.

The result was the development of new 'heavy' fuels, almost as dense as diesel and rich with aromatic compounds, with the aim of containing more 'energy' within the same volume.

Braking in Formula 1

"On the limit braking .... wheels blocked .... at the pit-stop, carbon dust comes out of the brakes ...."

These are just a few of the phrases that you will maybe hear during the television commentary of a GP. And the commentators, especially if they are ex-F1 drivers, often mention 'that once we used to brake 100 metres before".

It's true. Today's F1 brakes give performance that a few years ago was totally unimaginable but they have very little in common with those used in production cars.

This is mainly because the braking systems of F1 cars use carbon-fibre discs that reach their best performance at a 'working' temperature of between 450 and 600 degrees centigrade.

Those fitted to Ferrari, Benetton, Jordan, Minardi, Prost and Sauber are made up of callipers supplied by the Italian Brembo company, together with six pistons, two aluminium alloy pads and carbon-fibre discs that are 2.8 cm thick and 27.8 cm in diameter.

This is today; back in 1975, when Brembo started collaborating with

In order to increase the density of the fuel even further, and therefore cover more kilometres with the same amount of fuel, some teams used to cool it down to a temperature of minus 30°C before refuelling.

This was a major risk if the start was delayed, because in warm temperatures the fuels increased in volume and leaked from the pipes.

Further changes came about in 1988. After the turbo era, Ferrari went back to normally-aspirated engines (V12, 3500 cc) which took part in the following year's F1 championship.

Agip also had to take suitable measures. Normally-aspirated engines used oxygen-rich fuels that partly compensated for the elimination of the turbo.

Again with the collaboration of experts in the field of special rocket-fuel, Agip embarked on the search for new high-energy content molecules. The fuels were no longer produced and tested in refineries, but in their own research company (Euron), which was equipped with engine test rooms and energy experts.

As a result, fuels with an extremely pungent smell were produced, and the odour was so strong that they had to be made 'sweeter' with perfumed essences.

It was an endless technological race, with investments into research that often went far beyond the returns in terms of image or eventual commercial use.

And so we come to the present day, when, due to the new regulations totally banning the use of chemical

substances in fuels and limiting the possibility of developing new fuel formulas for F1, research by fuel companies is heavily penalised and as a result there has been a drop in interest and therefore investment in the sector.

1) A complete braking system from 1982. Disc in cast-iron, 4-piston caliper in aluminium and brake master cylinder.

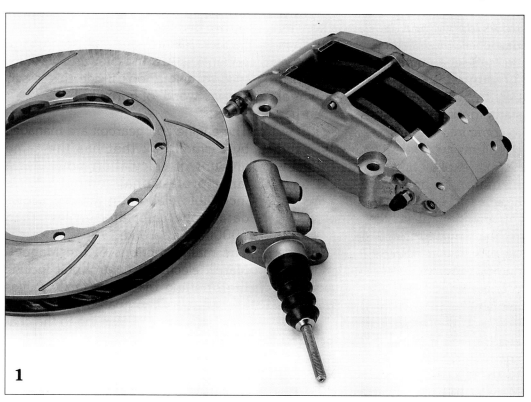

1

Ferrari, brakes were self-ventilated and in cast-iron, an alloy that is still used for production cars.

In order to reduce the weight of the brakes and the car in general, half-way through the 1980s major research went into developing a material that under stress would produce the best possible performance. This led to the use of carbon-fibre.

With carbon-fibre the weight went down from 6.6 kg for a braking system with cast-iron discs to 4.2 kg. And performance?

Just to give an idea, the table below compares the braking distance of a production car, with cast-iron disc brakes, with a carbon-fibre disc F1 car.

2) Carbon-fibre disc and 4-piston caliper from 1988.

3) 6-piston monoblock disc of a 1998 F1 car.

100 Kmh,	42 mt.	26 mt.
150 Kmh,	92 mt.	54 mt.
200 Kmh,	160 mt.	86 mt.

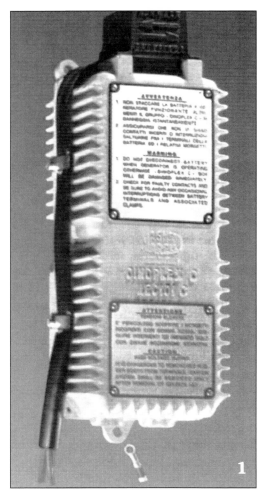

Electronics and telemetry

11 April 1999 - During the Brazilian GP, Hakkinen suddenly slows down and is overtaken by Barrichello and Schumacher but then starts to set a number of fastest laps.

27 June 1999 - During the French GP, Schumacher's steering-wheel starts to play up and the German has to come into the pits to replace it.

Problems with electronics was the laconic explanation of the TV commentator, in both cases. The term appears to be on everyone's lips yet this component (which is not visible for the TV spectator) is the nerve centre of a F1 car because it controls the engine, the fuel injection and gear changes. Electronics also manage data and information from the engine as well as many other parts of the car, and transmit it to the pit garage at the end of every lap.

With the assistance of Magneti Marelli, the company which has been alongside Ferrari since it was created and which today is partner not only of Ferrari but also of Williams, Benetton, Sauber, Minardi and, for some components, BAR and Stewart, we have tried to take a look inside this lesser-known 'world' of Formula 1.

The engine and gearbox are managed by a small box that has the same amount of calculation power as a large professional computer. This incredible elaboration speed allows data to be calculated in less than 1000th of a second.

The main functions of the Magneti Marelli electronic control unit include the opening of the butterfly valves according to a prepared programme and personalised according to the characteristics of that particular circuit and the different style of each driver. Basically it acts as a filter between the throttle and the opening of the butter-

fly valves. Even when the driver changes gear, the ECU intervenes, verifying that the 'request' made by the driver is compatible with the revs regime and the speed of the car.

Telemetry

Each time a car passes the pits, the ECU 'downloads' all the data it has collected during the lap, not only from the engine and gearbox, but also the data gathered from sensors located in many other parts of the car.

Temperature and pressure of the water and oil, of the engine and gearbox in different points, brake and tyre wear and fuel consumption are just some of the data that the box receives on each lap which is immediately compared with the team's 'control' data.

By means of this data, team personnel can keep an eye on the car lap after lap and can even decide race strategy according to tyre wear or fuel consumption.

*1) The precursor
of the modern-day ECU,
a DINOPLEX from 1968,
the first electronic starting unit
produced by Marelli.*

*2) A Magneti Marelli ECU
fitted to the leading F1 cars.
It measures 18 x 21 x 5 cms
and weighs just 2 kgs but has
a calculation power equivalent
to a professional computer.*

*3) A steering-wheel
made by Ferrari in collaboration
with Magneti Marelli and Momo.*

The search for safety

Talking about safety in a sport that is dominated by a continuous, exasperated quest for performance, and where the basic raw material is a racing-car and therefore a prototype, might appear to be almost absurd.

At every moment, racing teams and manufacturers of components present innovations that change the performance and the reactions of cars and as a result precautions to be adopted in case of incident also undergo changes.

The truth is that simulations are often not sufficient to introduce new safety standards and unfortunately it is incidents that highlight the defects and therefore the possible solutions.

To give an example of how often car development has forced 'safety' to follow a certain evolutionary path to make up ground, just think of guard-rails, which were erected to prevent cars from going off the circuit. In the 1960s, as F1 cars became wedge-shaped, the guard-rails became 'guillotines' and were therefore replaced with tyre walls. Or this year's introduction of a retention cable to prevent spectators, following drivers or even the driver of the car itself being hit by wayward wheels after accidents.

Another example is when circuits created wide grassy run-off areas around the track and on the outside of corners, which in the rain, were turned into terrifying 'mud-slides' for cars, 'torpedoing' them into the crash-barriers. Run-off areas were then modified and grass was replaced with sand or gravel.

One thing is certain, and it is that circuits, cars and driver clothing have all undergone major evolution over the years in the quest for improvements in both active and passive safety. To illustrate these changes, let us take a trip back in time to a Grand Prix Sunday ten years ago.

Imola

SAN MARINO GP
23 APRIL 1989

It's 2.37 p.m. The Grand Prix is into its fourth lap and the cars still have a full fuel load, when one of them enters the Tamburello curve, suddenly veers to the right and like a bullet, slams into the external wall at 280 kph, exploding in a ball of flames.

It was the Ferrari of Austrian driver Gerhard Berger, who remained unconscious in his cockpit surrounded by flames.

The next instant, first one and then two more men clothed in red holding extinguishers appeared from nowhere to douse the inferno with 18 kilograms of powder.

Later, after seeing the film again, we realised that just 14 seconds had passed between the moment of impact and the arrival of the first fire crews and 23 until the flames were put out completely.

Berger was pulled out of the car alive! He remained unconscious for three more minutes but incredibly he got away with just a few burns on the palm of his hand and a fractured shoulder-bone.

These injuries were nothing in comparison with the seriousness of the incident, the violence of the flames and the impact against the wall.

For this chapter on safety, we wanted to start with Berger's crash at Imola, which had a happy ending, allowing the Austrian to get back behind the wheel in Mexico after missing just two GPs.

Berger was clearly lucky, due to a set of favourable circumstances but on that occasion we were also faced with the proof that a lot has been done to improve both active and passive safety in Formula 1.

The car had been built with the first 'safety cells', it was fitted with 5-point safety belts which stood up to the tremendous impact, keeping the driver firmly anchored to his seat, Berger was wearing a fire-proof suit and finally the fire crews intervened rapidly and efficiently.

Unfortunately even in recent Formula 1 history, other incidents have not had the same positive conclusion, but it is clear that safety has improved from year to year.

Anti-spill fuel tanks, increasingly fire-resistant race suits, wider cockpits with better side protection and larger run-off areas will all be soon accompanied with lights indicating danger situations to drivers, special tarmac that allows immediate drainage after thunderstorms and highly-absorbent protective barriers at the side of the track ... as well as many other developments.

The men out of ... nowhere

The men who saved the life of Gerhard Berger form part of the 200 members of Imola's team of 'CEA Squadra Corse' safety marshalls. Then, as now, they are present in Italy's leading circuits, but not only there.

The volunteers of the organisation founded in 1970 by Ermete Amadesi, the owner of CEA Fire Extinguishers, were at the time called the 'three CEA lions'. The aim was to form a group of professionally-trained men prepared to tackle fire emergencies. CEA provided the material and assistance and developed and organised theoretical and practical training courses.

In addition, the organisation provides fire-fighting services for the leading Italian and European circuits, as well as sending experts throughout the world and holding courses about all aspects of fire-fighting. One could almost say that CEA marshalls are directly present in many circuits today, and where they are not, there is in any case a bit of CEA.

Today the CEA Squadra Corse has more than 300 specialists, together with 40 rapid-intervention cars and 23 off-road 4wd vehicles equipped with the latest fire-fighting equipment and two special vehicles with cutting equipment to intervene and rapidly pull the driver out of the cockpit.

But the cornerstones of the organisation, now as then, are the 'men in red', all volunteers, all with their usual jobs during the week, who become 'guardian angels' on the side of the track at the weekend, and who are compensated for their work with hospitality and modest expenses and with a dream ... that of never having to intervene in case of fire.

Circuit safety

At Imola, during the San Marino GP, the CEA Squadra Corse is responsible for the fire-fighting service. The following is the equipment they set up at the circuit for the three-day event, at trackside but also in the pits, the paddock and areas reserved for helicopters:
* 200 men with fire-fighting suits and helmets, each with a 6 kg portable fire-extinguisher (one marshall approximately every 50 metres).

* 76 fire-extinguishers (50 kg) on trolleys positioned along the circuit.
* 16 rapid-intervention cars, each containing 7 portable fire-extinguishers (6 kg) and 2 fixed extinguishers (60 kg).

* 16 4wd off-road vehicles, each containing 3 fixed extinguishers and 6 portable ones.
* 2 multi-function vehicles with special cutting equipment to intervene and pull the driver out of the cockpit.

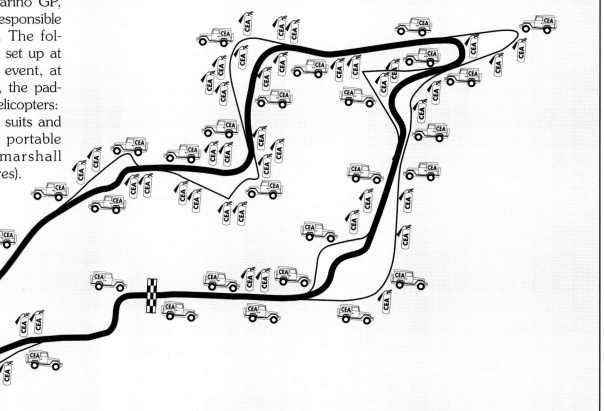

A suit is born

On Monday 12th July Mika Salo was called to Ferrari and the next day he signed a deal to drive Schumacher's car until the German returned. Then, with a race suit borrowed from Irvine, he got into the legendary number 3 Ferrari for the first time for a few laps. On Thursday he was out on the track again with a brand-new, flame-red race suit, this time created especially for the Finn and bearing his name. How was this possible?

The answer comes from OMP, the Italian firm that supplies Ferrari drivers (as well as Barrichello and, in the past, the legendary Senna) with their race wear, in addition to the Maranello refuelling mechanics.

All that was necessary was a fax with Salo's measurements to set in motion the race division of OMP and in two days three suits were ready for the

smallish Finn. Others would follow in the next few days.

A driver like Schumacher for example uses about 30 race suits in a year, between testing and racing, in several different liveries, with or without cigarette logos.

The suits are created in triple-layer Nomex: eight hours of work and more than 7 metres of material are required both inside and out, with the sponsor logos (also in the same fireproof material) either stitched or stuck on. The total weight of each suit is around 1.5 kg.

Berger's suit

From a yellow shirt and blue trousers, the traditional race overalls of Tazio Nuvolari in the 1940s, to suits in cotton poplin treated on the surface with a fireproof spray in the 1960s, to the fire resistant race suit, underwear and gloves of the drivers of today, progress has been enormous; ten years ago, in the Imola inferno, Berger was wearing a triple-layer suit, underwear in fire-resistant material - Nomex, manufactured by Dupont - in addition to gloves in the same material.

It was the gloves that were the weak link in the extraordinarily efficient protection against fire. In fact, either because the gloves were made of thinner material than the suit, or because the fire penetrated through the stitches that hold the chamois leather on the palms, it was Berger's hands that had the worst burns.

It is worth mentioning that for Imola, as reported by the newspapers of the time, Berger himself had asked OMP, the Italian company that supplies him with his race suit, to make him a high-protection version and he had agreed to OMP's suggestion to wear an body suit instead of the normal cotton T-shirt he had always used.

This oversight could have cost him dearly because at the temperatures reached during the fire, the cotton would have burst into flames and melted to the skin, causing unthinkable damage.

Yet a few years before, narrow F1 cockpits had led many drivers to wear thinner, lighter suits offering less protection, in order to have a bit more movement or to feel cooler inside their suits.

Since Berger's accident, driver race suits have not changed that much and the most commonly used material today is still Nomex. Changes have been made in the design, the protection of the stitches and in the application of shoulder straps to enable the driver to be pulled out of the cockpit.

What has changed is the drivers themselves, who are more aware of safety and therefore more committed to implementing it in collaboration with companies producing safety accessories.

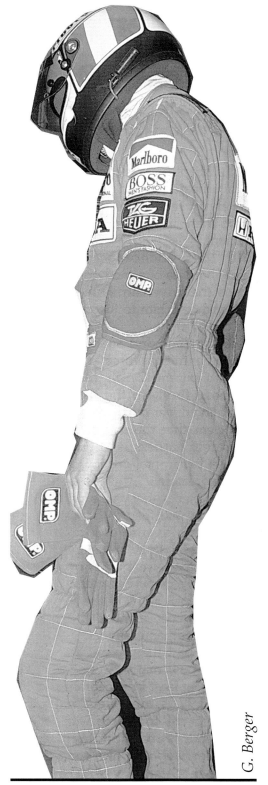

G. Berger

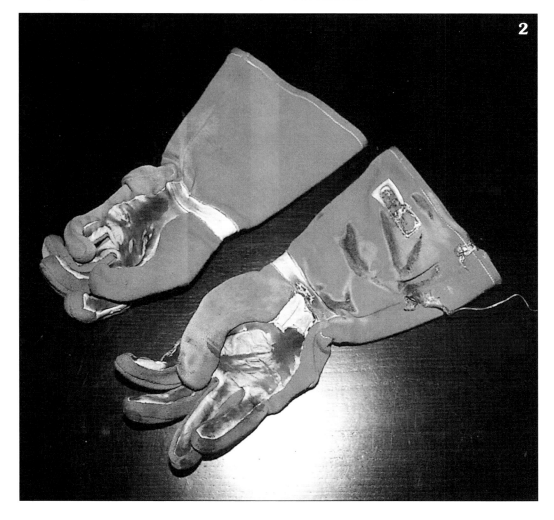

1) Race-suit manufacture. In the foreground one of Ayrton Senna's suits with sponsors' logos.

2) In the photo, Berger's gloves after his incident at Imola in 1989. Note the palms of the gloves that did not stand up so well to the fire, leading to his hands being burnt.

Gentlemen.. fasten your seatbelts!

In this chapter we take a look at seatbelt harnesses, which for a Formula 1 driver represent something rather more than just protection in case of incident.

With its 6 anchorage points, the safety harness of a modern-day F1 car keeps the driver firmly in his racing seat and help him to 'become' part of the car.

In fast curves and sudden braking, where centrifugal force and deceleration are extremely high, the belts hold the body firmly in the seat, without restricting driver movement.

It is clear that the major function of the safety harness is in case of incident, either frontal or more frequently in racing, lateral.

The six pieces that make up the harness allow the load to be distributed more evenly in case of incident, thus protecting the body of the driver.

In F1, seatbelts were made compulsory by the International Federation in 1972 but even back in 1968 the Federation itself had recommended their use to single-seater manufacturers.

Over the past thirty years, there have not been any major developments in seatbelts, at least in appearance.

In the 1970s they were narrower (around 5 cm compared with today's 7 cm) but were manufactured in polyester webbing like today. The release mechanism was different to today and not as rapid, and above all the harness was 4 point not 6 point.

The release mechanism, particularly in an emergency, must allow the driver to undo the six harness points with one rapid twist of the buckle. Today's regulations in fact stipulate that a driver must be able to release the harness, get out of the cockpit and remove the steering wheel in 10 seconds.

The fabric used in F1 seatbelts has to have a breaking-point of close to 4500 kg, almost double that of a normal seatbelt.

It must be pointed out that in Schumacher's incident at Silverstone,

1

100

the frontal impact subjected the driver to a deceleration force of close to 25G, despite the tyre barrier. To give a better idea, US Space Shuttle pilots are subjected to a maximum acceleration of 'only' 6G when they are launched into space.

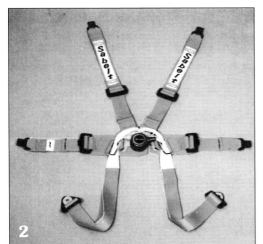

1) For more than 15 years, Jean Todt, Ferrari Sporting Director since 1993, was co-driver to several rally champions.

2) F1 1999 seat-belt by SABELT.

3) The 1979 Alfa Romeo of Bruno Giacomelli, the first car to fit seat-belts manufactured by SABELT, today the official supplier to Ferrari.

4) Brazil's Nelson Piquet, 1987 World Champion with Williams.

The Ferrari team manager's meat sauce

Can you imagine Jean Todt slaving in front of a hot stove between a couple of qualifying sessions, avidly preparing a nice plate of spaghetti bolognese for the team mechanics and drivers? It would be pure fantasy ...

Yet some time ago, you could see this sort of thing in F1. Back in the 1970s, you could bump into Franco Gozzi, Ferrari team manager and Enzo Ferrari's right-hand man, who after unloading a gas stove from the team truck, would immediately start preparing a pasta sauce.

This is just one of the many memories of two Ferrari mechanics of those years, Gisberto Leopardi and Sergio Vezzali, both Ferrari employees for more than 35 years, and for a long time mechanics in the F1 and Sports-Prototype teams.

Those were the years when teams were

made up of no more than 10 mechanics: one for the engine, one for the gearbox, four for tyres and refuelling and two 'all-purpose' mechanics, usually younger. The final mechanic was also the driver of the truck that transported the cars, equipment and spare parts from race to race. He would also be responsible for pit-wall signalling, hanging out the boards during qualifying and the race.

Like the legendary Pignatti, driver at the time of Surtees, Bandini and Parkes.

One year he left Maranello for the British GP and arrived at the Mont Blanc tunnel, only to find it shut.

No problem. He turned round, headed for Montecarlo, then Lyon, crossed France, arrived in Calais and got on the ferry-boat to go to Brands Hatch.

These were never-ending journeys, departure would be immediately after the race with the trucks of the time, full of spare parts as well as Lambrusco wine, tortellini and ham, carefully hidden to get through customs which did not allow the import of foodstuffs into the northern European countries.

When Grand Prixs involved trips overseas, the red trucks bearing the Ferrari logo were replaced with ships and cargo aircraft.

Both Leopardi and Vezzali still remember the journey to the USA in 1970 for the Daytona 24 Hour sports-prototype race.

A British cargo plane was there to meet them at Rome's Fiumicino airport, with the cars already loaded. The men from Maranello were asked to get on board the plane and they found themselves having to sit on makeshift seats installed immediately behind the cars themselves.

The flight was all at low altitude with constant turbulence until a technical

stop-over at Gander on the island of Newfoundland. Here they had a short stop in a hangar for a cup of hot tea while outside, temperatures hovered around -30°C, then it was back in the plane for the final leg to Florida.

The race itself was on that famous concrete track with a rough surface that caused incredible vibrations to the cars. Half-way through the race, the Ferrari of Andretti broke the front end of the chassis and returned to the pits. In 40 minutes it was welded back together as well as possible by the mechanics led by Mauro Forghieri. When he was about to get back in the car, Andretti asked: "What were the repairs like?". "Like putting a plaster on a broken leg" replied the mechanic.

Andretti went back out again, not entirely reassured, and took the Ferrari to 3rd place overall after a fantastic recovery.

These are just a few anecdotes that belong to a world that is so far removed from the one experienced today, a world that united drivers, mechanics and engineers in a rapport that was one of trust but also real friendship. Like in 1970 when Clay Regazzoni won at Monza in a Ferrari and was

1) Franco Gozzi
with Niki Lauda and Borsari.

2) Sergio Vezzali today
in a photograph and in 1968
together with Enzo Ferrari.

3) The Ferrari team getting ready
for the start. From left to right: a
young Leopardi, the famous chief
mechanic Borsari, truck driver and
pit wall signal mechanic Pignatti,
and Frigerio, gearbox mechanic.

surrounded by journalists and reporters who wanted to interview him and get him to appear on the various sports programmes on TV.

"I'm sorry, this evening I can't come. If you want, you can catch me at the Sant'Eustorgio restaurant near the circuit, because I'm having dinner with my mechanics".

Or at Montecarlo in 1966, when Lorenzo Bandini, after finishing second behind Jackie Stewart, decided to give his mechanics all his prize-money and, for the first time ever, brought them along to the party at the Hotel de Paris.

United in joy but also in tragedy, such as in 1971 when the mechanics wanted to bring back from Argentina the coffin containing Ignazio Giunti, who was killed in an incredible incident in the Buenos Aires 1000 kms race.

Or when Sergio Vezzali waited in vain for the Ferrari of Gilles Villeneuve at the Zolder circuit in Belgium on that fateful 8th May 1982.

Gisberto Leopardi today with the tools used by a Ferrari mechanic of the time.

Modern-day Grand Prix preparation

For Ferrari, preparation for a Grand Prix begins many weeks before, with flights and hotel bookings for the approximately 60 people who make up the team.

The next job on the list is the preparation of a small booklet for that particular GP, containing all the necessary information: type of team clothing that must be worn (if cigarette logos are permitted or not), list of persons going to the GP with mobile phone numbers, hotels used for the GP, timetable of briefings, recommended restaurants nearby, useful phone numbers, etc.

Each person going to the GP, from Jean Todt right down to the team personnel,

receives one of these booklets. The 59-strong Ferrari team is made up of:

22 mechanics
8 technicians
10 engineers
12 logistics staff

plus the 2 drivers, their managers, the press officer and the team manager. This small army arrives at each Grand Prix preceded by three large trucks for the cars, the spare parts and everything that is required by the Technical Division and the workshop as well as two smaller trucks with the tools and team decor.

In addition there are two splendid motorhomes that are used as operations headquarters for the team manager and the drivers as well as one for the press office and hospitality unit for journalists. All this makes up almost 20 tons of material which travels from circuit to circuit in Europe. It becomes more than 25 when the race is overseas due to the special crates used to protect cars and equipment.

Approximately 60 people distributed between paddock and pits, in permanent contact with each other via a network of 'walkie-talkies' that they never abandon for one instant until the chequered flag marks the end of each GP.

Once upon a time ... there was Formula 1

There was a time when if you walked around the paddock (at one time you could!), you might bump into Alessandro Nannini (Minardi), smoking a cigarette, whiling away the time between qualifying sessions by playing cards with Michele Alboreto (Ferrari). Just a few yards away, in the Minardi garage, a young lady with needle and thread might be sewing the logo of a new sponsor onto the drivers' race suits.

You might even have met Riccardo Patrese, taking his children to the motorhome for a rest, while in another motorhome Alain Prost in his underwear was getting ready to slip into his race suit for the next session.

That was the time when Nelson Piquet fooled around on the podium or used to embarrass the Italian TV journalist interviewing him by saying the occasional swear word live from his cockpit before the start of the race.

Even Ferrari mechanics could enjoy a few brief moments of fun with 'piggy' masks or have a drink of excellent Lambrusco wine with their meals. On the subject of Lambrusco, as soon as he arrived at Ferrari, John Barnard tried to 'ban' the habit of drinking wine for the Ferrari mechanics, almost leading to the first alcohol-based strike in F1!

High-tech equipment and sophisticated decor had not yet turned pit garages into the magnificent structures they are today; a box to sit on and one for the timing monitor was all that was required by a great engineer such as Carlo Chiti to follow practice or qualifying.

The general public were closer to their heroes and one enterprising person even managed to get onto the track dressed up as a racing-driver.

Once upon a time, all this was possible ... and that was only 1987, just over 10 years ago.

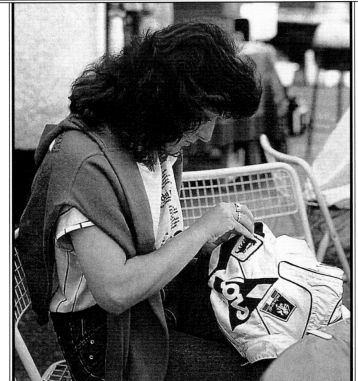

Photo Daniele Amaduzzi 1986

Formula 1

1950-1999

When the Formula 1 World Championship began in spring 1950, few people could have imagined that motorsport's most prestigious category was going to be such a world-wide success.

Every year Formula 1 captures the attention of billions of TV viewers around the world. It is a global television spectacle that is on a similar level to the Olympic Games. The Olympics however only come round once every four years ...

Hundreds of pages would be needed just to summarise the most important facts, characters and technical developments that have characterised the past fifty years of Formula 1. It would be an encyclopaedia, therefore we will just trace a brief outline of each decade with the salient facts and most significant events.

THE 1950S

Hostilities got underway at Silverstone in March 1950 with the same cars that had given rise to numerous exciting duels on the eve of the Second World War. The cars were gigantic, single-seater, front wheel drive, supercharged, heavy to drive and even more difficult to keep on the road. They were dangerous cars that were mastered by a brilliant driver: Juan Manuel Fangio. The Argentinean was the only man in the history of Formula 1 to win five world titles, for Alfa Romeo, Mercedes, Ferrari and Maserati. He was a champion who had no peers, but also a master of strategy, a driver whose destiny on the track was always linked with the best cars of the time.

The 1950s were also characterised by the birth of a new legend: Ferrari. In just a few years, the new Italian manufacturer came to the attention of the general public thanks to a series of victories ... and world titles. Like the ones won by Ascari in 1952 and 1953, by Fangio in 1956 and by Hawthorn in 1958.

THE 1960S

The new decade got underway with the definitive success of rear-wheeled cars and the triumphant return of Ferrari. In 1961 the Maranello manufacturer again won the world title with American Phil Hill and Enzo Ferrari grudgingly had to abandon "... the horses that pulled the cart" and convert to those who "... pushed it".

The Italian manufacturer was forced to follow the innovation of the rear engine introduced by Cooper in 1959. This was an authentic technological revolution that brought about the creation of a new kind of car, with its engine in the rear, low centre of gravity and the driver almost lying down.

This type of car construction led to the rise of the British manufacturers, who were skilful in building lightweight but extremely rigid chassis. A fine example of this was the monocoque chassis introduced in 1963 by Colin Chapman on the legendary Lotus 25/33. This car was a revolution and created an abyss between the 'assemblers' from over the Channel and Ferrari of Italy, the undisputed leader in the engine sector.

The Lotus 25/33 was an authentic milestone in the technical evolution of Grand Prix racing, and became identified more than anyone else with the Scottish driver Jim Clark, who became the symbol of the 1960s and a worthy successor to Juan Manuel Fangio.

THE 1970S

Every era is characterised by one or more drivers and by the technical developments on the cars of the period. This was not the case in the 1970s, which was a decade of great technical ferment, difficult to identify with one particular method of construction. At least three innovations characterised the cars of this period: the aerodynamic revolution, the arrival of the turbo and skirts. Let us proceed in order. At the end of the 1960s, the introduction of the first wings, fitted to the 1968 Ferrari 312, brought about the creation of cars that were substantially different to the 'cigar-shaped' cars of the 1960s.

It was discovered that as well as engine/car performance, it was also important to have good downforce (negative downward air pressure), which gave better adherence to the ground and higher cornering speeds. This led to the proliferation of wings, a development that was followed by the introduction of the wedge shape and the Tyrrell six-wheeled car in 1976/77. Those years also saw the debut in F1 of the Renault turbo. The arrival of the French manufacturer in the Grand Prix world was greeted everywhere with great scepticism. It was considered that turbo engines were far too penalised in comparison with normally-aspirated engines. The decade that followed demonstrated the contrary ...

The third and final technical revolution was the so-called 'wing-car'. This exploited the particular conformation of the underside of the car to generate an impressive amount of downforce. The 1970s, characterised by 'computer-drivers' of the calibre of Stewart and Lauda, were also those of a massive increase in the number of sponsors in motorsport and the profound transformation of F1 from an almost amateurish category into a sporting phenomenon of world-wide importance.

THE 1980S

The turbo engine, mocked by many on its debut in F1, took its revenge. The performance and the power of turbo-charged engines through turbines and compressors increased exponentially. From the 500 bhp of the 1977 Renault, they reached the more than 1200 bhp of the 4 cylinder BMW unit that powered Nelson Piquet's 1985 Brabham BT54. This was an extraordinary figure, one that required even greater physical effort and mental concentration from drivers. The figure of the latter also underwent a profound transformation in the ten-year period from the mid-80s onwards.

The death of Gilles Villeneuve, considered to be the last-ever risk-taker behind the wheel, marked the birth of a new breed of champion. Scrupulous drivers became careful managers of their own activities and their physical training. They became top-flight sportsmen, who were in no way inferior to specialists from other disciplines.

The prototype of this new breed of driver was Ayrton Senna. The unforgettable Brazilian champion was not only a symbol of the latest generation of drivers, but he was also probably even the best driver of all time. Senna was an extraordinary champion who accompanied meticulous, almost maniacal preparation with an instinctive and extraordinarily efficient driving ability.

THE 1990S

This brief overview of F1 history comes to an end with the decade in course. It has been an intense period, tragically marked by the death of Ayrton Senna and the rise of a new idol: Michael Schumacher. Schumacher is also the symbol of a Formula 1 that is more impersonal, dominated by massive economic and financial interests and by the major constructors which, one by one, have taken over or are taking over all the old teams (except Ferrari). Too often, modern-day Formula 1 is a category dominated by electronics, light-years away from the worn-out stereotype of the old style of motorsport, but also far removed from the expectations of fans who are not always able to identify themselves with a sport that is becoming increasingly self-contained and accessible to just a few privileged 'insiders'.

1950
1959

1950

1951

1952

1953

114

1956

1957

1958

HAVOLINE

1959/60

1954/55

1961

1962

1963

TEAM LOTUS

1960

1969

1964

1965

1966

1967

1968

1969

1970
1979

1970

1972

1973

1974

1975

1976

1978

1977

1979

121

1980

1981

1982

1984

1983

122

1985/86

1980
1989

1987

1989

1988

1990
1999

1990

1991

1993

1992

1994

126

1997

1995

1996

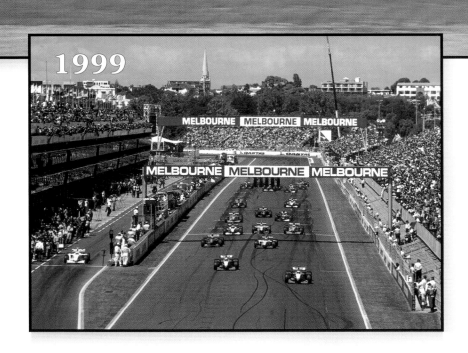

1999

1998

McLAREN - MERCEDES MP4/14

SAUBER - PETRONAS C18

FERRARI F399

BAR - SUPERTEC 01

WILLIAMS - SUPERTEC FW21

PROST - PEUGEOT AP02

BENETTON - SUPERTEC B199

ARROWS A19

JORDAN - MUGEN HONDA 199

MINARDI - FORD M01

STEWART - FORD SF-3

FERRARI F399

FORMULA 1 1999: TECHNICAL FOCUS

by Paolo D'Alessio

Unpredictable, irrational, surprising, puzzling. These are just a few of the adjectives that could be used to describe the 1999 Formula 1 Championship.

This year will certainly not go down in history for the technical developments made by the various teams. It will be remembered however for the events that characterised it and for the upsets it produced. In short, the championship was spectacular and exciting but rather low-key on a technical level.

At the start of the year, it had seemed that the 1999 championship was going to be dominated by McLaren. After Australian GP qualifying, the Angle-German team appeared to be even stronger than the previous year. But it proved to be a 'flash in the pan', which fizzled out after the first third of the race with the retirement of both the silver cars of Coulthard and Hakkinen. With respect to last year, the MP4-14 had improved in performance, it had become more sophisticated, aerodynamically and mechanically more refined, and surprisingly lighter and more compact ... but less reliable.

As often happens in Formula 1, Adrian Newey had suffered from 'winner's syndrome', a sort of omnipotent frenzy that afflicts geniuses who are unable to rest on their laurels and who constantly want to make their creations more competitive. They are eccentric geniuses who complicate their lives with their own hands. It is a well-known fact that in Formula 1 the search for perfection and excessive technical exasperation produce problems rather than concrete results. Troubled with unreliability and unexpected breakages, the car that should have dominated the 1999 season ended up by opening the doors to other, less fancied contenders, Ferrari above all.

In a position that was in direct contrast to McLaren, the Maranello manufacturer was once again counting on reliability and constant performance being the key factors in its championship challenge.

These two demands ended up by heavily conditioning the F399 project and Ferrari lined up against the technically-exasperated McLaren with a much more traditional car.

The saving grace for Ferrari was the fact that the best qualities of the F399 were its constant performance and progressive improvement. It was a pity however that Ferrari's season was conditioned by the events in Malaysia, the incident of Michael Schumacher at Silverstone and the errors at the Nurburgring. The absence of the German champion had a major effect on the development of the red cars and prevented them from aspiring to the role of leader, which with the McLarens in difficulty, could have easily been achieved.

As mentioned before, the setbacks for the Prancing Horse team and the varying performance of the McLarens opened the doors to other teams. The ones to emerge were Jordan and Stewart, two teams to keep an eye on, not so much for their 1999 performance but in a future prospective. Eddie Jordan's team because it has become a concrete reality in modern-day F1 and because in 2000 it can count on even more direct support from Honda.

Stewart because, after just three years in the F1 circus, it has entered into the Ford orbit and from next year onwards will race under the Jaguar-Ford banner. On the other hand, Benetton, BAR, Prost and Williams were a complete disappointment. The team that dominated F1 in the early '90s ran aground, and things were only salvaged by the ever-improving performances of Ralf Schumacher. Next year will see the arrival of BMW engines, but the learning curve for the German engine manufacturer promises to be long and difficult.

Benetton and Prost are looking ahead to an even murkier future. The Anglo-Italian team will have to be completely revamped if it wants to get back to the top again, while the Prost has highlighted the total failure of the Peugeot project in F1.

Finally, the end of year balance-sheet for BAR was a total disaster. The Anglo-American team was supposed to set the F1 world alight, according to its managers and its ambitious and generous sponsor, but instead only made the headlines for continuous breakages and the two-coloured livery on the cars of Villeneuve and Zonta.

McLaren

Once again McLaren-Mercedes produced the best car on the grid and the reference point for everyone else. The MP4-14 dominated the 1999 season but maybe did not perform up to the usual high standards in terms of results and victories. This was due to opponents that proved to be tougher than expected, reliability that was not up to standard and an inexplicable series of mistakes along the way. Had it not been for all this, the MP4-14 would probably have been the first car in the history of F1 to win every round. Let's proceed in order. The 1999 world championship got underway in Australia with a McLaren that was much faster than expected, and in qualifying the gap to Schumacher's Ferrari was around one-and-a-half seconds. In the race however both Hakkinen and Coulthard were forced to retire. The situation could have been the same in Brazil had the electronics of car number 1 not started to function again after a sudden unexpected black-out. The reason for all this was plain for all to see. Adrian Newey, the engineering wizard for the Ron Dennis-run team, had not merely been content with improving the '98 championship-winning car. He had wanted to revolutionise it and refine it wherever possible, exasperating the aerodynamics, the weight distribution and the suspension systems as much as possible ...... with a risk of overloading a series of smaller-sized components. As if all that were not enough, once the technical problems had been sorted out and the MP4-14 made reliable, the McLaren team itself threw a spanner in the works. The 1999 season saw the squad in major difficulty: Hakkinen's wheel fell off at Silverstone, pit-stops were chaotic, Hakkinen and Coulthard occasionally had an all-McLaren battle, culminating in contact at Zeltweg and Spa. Not to mention the world champion's two 'strange' retirements at Imola and Monza, which cost the Finnish driver 20 vital points. In both circumstances, Hakkinen blamed himself, but well-founded suspicion remains that something else lay behind these outbursts of self-responsibility.

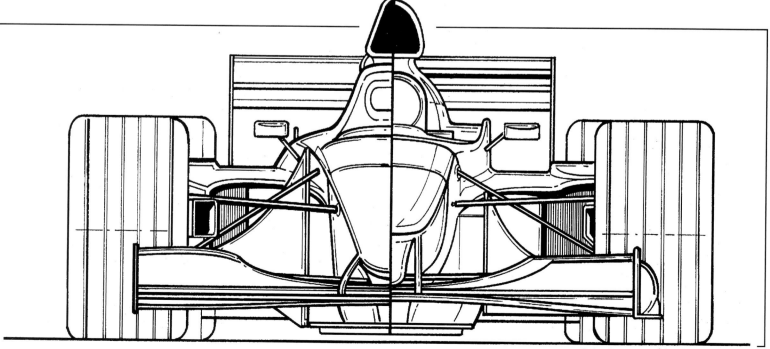

P. D'ALESSIO · 99 PD'A

If the '98 McLaren MP4-13
(see detail below)
and the MP4-14 are compared,
small but significant differences
can be seen between the two models.
The 1999 car has a different
sidepod design and the rear
of the car is much more tapered
(this can also be seen in the side
view of the MP4-14).
The nose is a different shape and
is slightly curved while the cockpit,
and as a result weight distribution,
is further back.
On the McLaren '99
the radiant masses have
also been moved further back.

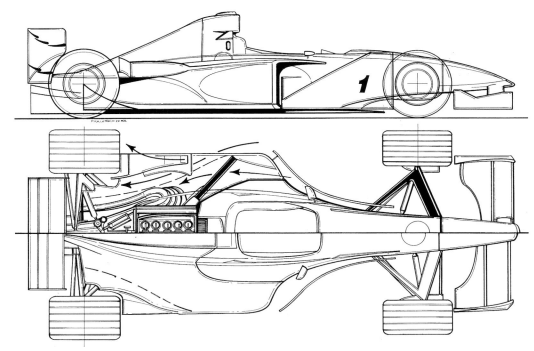

High nose or low nose?
While Ferrari again opted
for the former in 1999,
the world champion team
remained faithful to the solution
introduced last year by Adrian Newey
on the title-winning MP4-13.
As can be seen in the front view,
on the base version of the MP4-14,
the steering arm is high up,
with the struts sheathed
in the aerodynamic, wing-shaped,
carbon-fibre shroud that covers
the top wishbone.
Only half-way through
the season did Newey revert
to the system used last year,
with the steering arm lower down
the upright, a solution that,
according to the drivers,
improved the car's ride.
In the design below, the solution
used last year on the MP4-13,
recalled for the 1999 car.

The layout of the front suspension on the MP4-14
was substantially unchanged from last year's model.
The dampers are almost vertical and are activated
by a rocker arm that guarantees greater travel.
The torsion bars continue to be horizontal as on the MP4-13
and can be easily extracted from the front part of the body.
The function of the third damper, joined to the anti-roll bar,
is to reduce roll and pitch to a minimum.

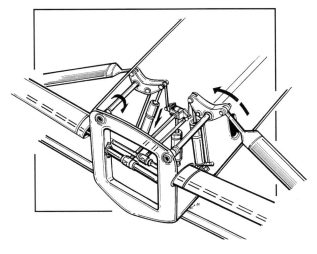

McLAREN MP4/13

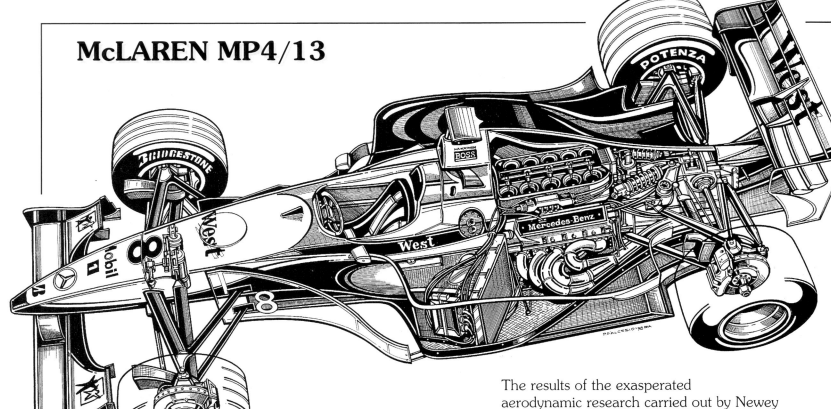

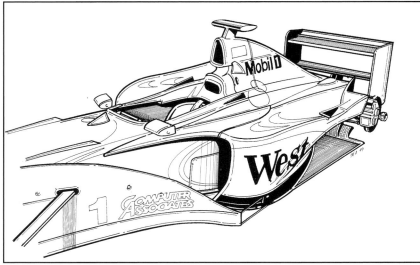

The results of the exasperated aerodynamic research carried out by Newey on the MP4-14 can be seen in this view of the side of Hakkinen's and Coulthard's cars. The entry is more rounded-off than the '98 car and is smaller in size. In order to reduce the dimensions of the sidepods to a minimum, several ECU on the MP4-14 are housed inside the chassis.

Even champions copy sometimes, as was the case of McLaren which looked to Ferrari for the design of its rear bodywork. With respect to the red cars, the side fins of the MP4-14 also had an exit for the hot air coming out of the sidepods. This exit had two purposes: deflect the flow of air over the rear wheels and reduce temperatures inside the engine bay.

The rear of the McLaren MP4-14 contains
a new suspension layout, characterised
by horizontal dampers and vertical torsion bars,
situated in front of the drive shaft.
As for the Ferrari, the adjustment of the bars
and the ground ride height on the McLaren
is also quite simple and is made easier
by the layout of the new suspension
and by the position of the torsion bars that can
easily be extracted from the upper part
of the transmission.

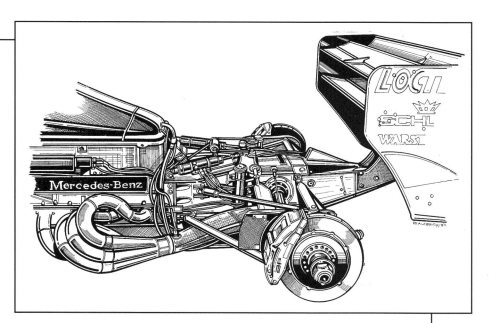

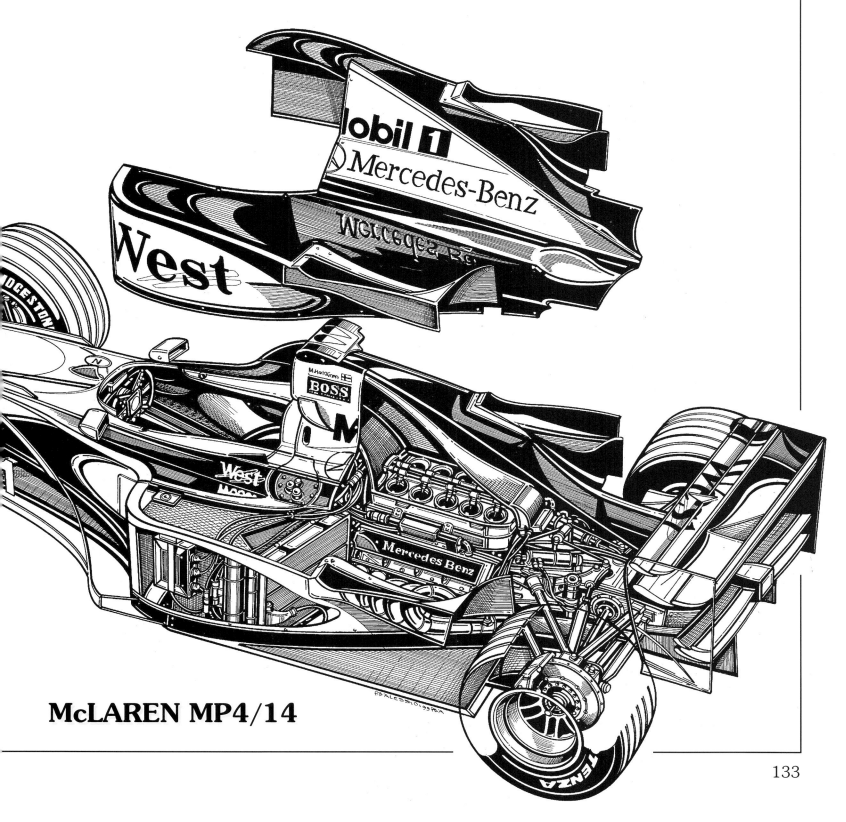

McLAREN MP4/14

FERRARI

Ferrari's 1999 season
was conditioned by two particular
episodes: Schumacher's incident
and affairs in McLaren.
We prefer to overlook the first point
because as always 'ifs' and 'buts'
and hypotheses and suppositions
are best left well alone.
History is not made with
recriminations but with facts.
The facts of 1999 tell us that once
again (for the twentieth successive
year) the Prancing Horse was forced
to play 'catch-up' to its rivals.
After the outcome of the winter tests,
at Maranello they were convinced
that the 1999 season would get
underway with Ferrari almost
on a level playing-field with
the world champions.
However the gap between the F399
and the McLaren in the first round
of the world championship soon
turned out to be alarming …
dramatic even.
Luckily it was Ferrari's rivals
themselves who gave a hand
to Irvine and Schumacher,
with a car that was sophisticated
and fast but just as fragile.
The unexpected wins in Australia
and at Imola were more a result
of McLaren's problems than
any particular merit.
The same could be said of Irvine's

lucky wins in Austria and Germany ,
where Ferrari's' only real merit was
to find itself in the right place
at the right time, that is behind
the McLarens when they suffered
a series of unexpected problems.
The only real triumph of the season
was the Monaco GP, where the
F399s of Schumacher and Irvine
were unbeatable. Montecarlo however
is famous for being a strange circuit,
where even an imperfect car can
dominate. Looking at the season
as a whole, the F399 was far from
perfect. It was too conservative,
according to some people,
to win the title on reliability alone.
According to others, its performance
deteriorated, unlike the McLarens
which after a difficult start to the
season, progressively improved.
With Schumacher in the team,
things would probably have
been different, but,
as we mentioned before,
history is not made of 'ifs'
and 'buts' … and neither is a
championship-winning Formula 1 car.

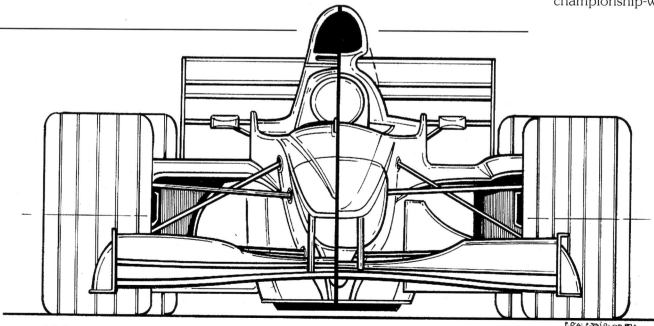

There were a number of differences between the 1998 and 1999 Ferraris. The F399 was characterised by having a more curvy shape and it was studied in order to improve the aerodynamics in the rear, where the bodywork had a marked tapering around the drive wheels and a small, clearly McLaren-inspired deflector that partially streamlined the rear. The design of the sides was cleaner than the 1998 car and did not contain any holes for the exit of the hot air from the radiant masses, which in the F399 was expelled through a small hole under the two small side deflectors.

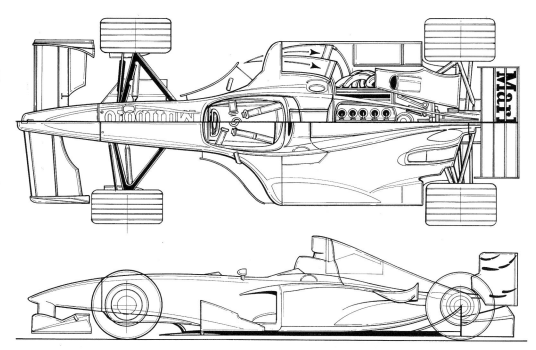

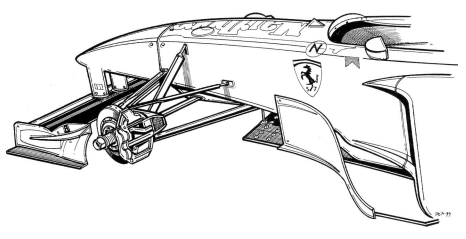

The front end of the 1999 Ferrari was virtually unchanged. The suspension was virtually the same as last year, even though on the front axle there was new electronically-controlled power steering. The nose had also been seen before. The F399's front wing was the same as the one used in the last two races of the 1998 season by Irvine and Schumacher and recalls the one used by Ferrari from 1974 onwards, first on the 312B3 and then on the legendary 312T.

At Imola the Ferrari nose assumed its definitive configuration. The race at the Santerno circuit in fact saw the debut of a new front wing, together with new endplates. The aim of the modifications was to improve air flow at the front and reduce front wheel 'interference' to a minimum.

The front suspension was virtually unchanged. With respect to last year, the position of the dampers was changed slightly and is now just off vertical and inwardly-slanting. The F399 also uses a third horizontal damper (for control of pitch and roll) and horizontal torsion bars, which can easily be extracted from the front part of the chassis. On the F399 the steering arm is placed lower down and is activated by a new electronically-controlled power steering unit. Both the front and rear suspensions of the Ferrari are the so-called 'counteractive' type.

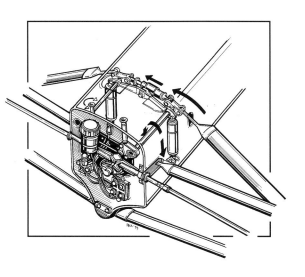

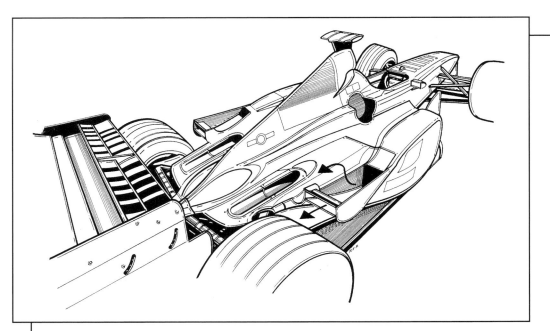

From the French GP onwards, a new bodywork appeared on the F399, with larger side fins and a hot air exit in front of the rear wheels. This solution, modified from the McLaren MP4-14, had a dual purpose: improve the air flow over the rear wing and lower the working temperatures inside the engine bay. For fast circuits, Ferrari also designed new smaller but extremely efficient rear wings (details on previous page). The one used at Hockenheim and Monza was characterised by being delta-shaped.

This was unusual for modern-day F1 but evoked similar devices used by Ferrari and others on a series of cars in the 1970s.

To be exact, the first delta-shaped wing made its debut in 1974 on the 312B3 of Niki Lauda and Clay Regazzoni.

FERRARI F 310

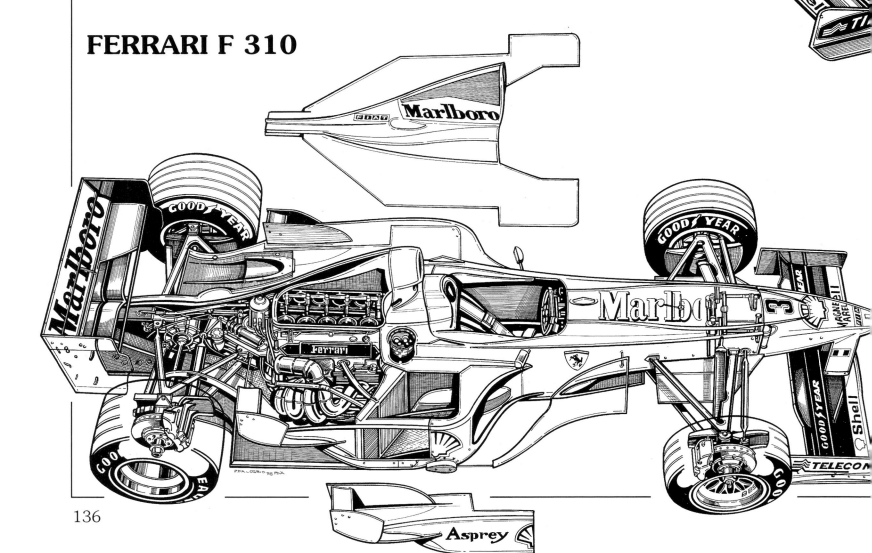

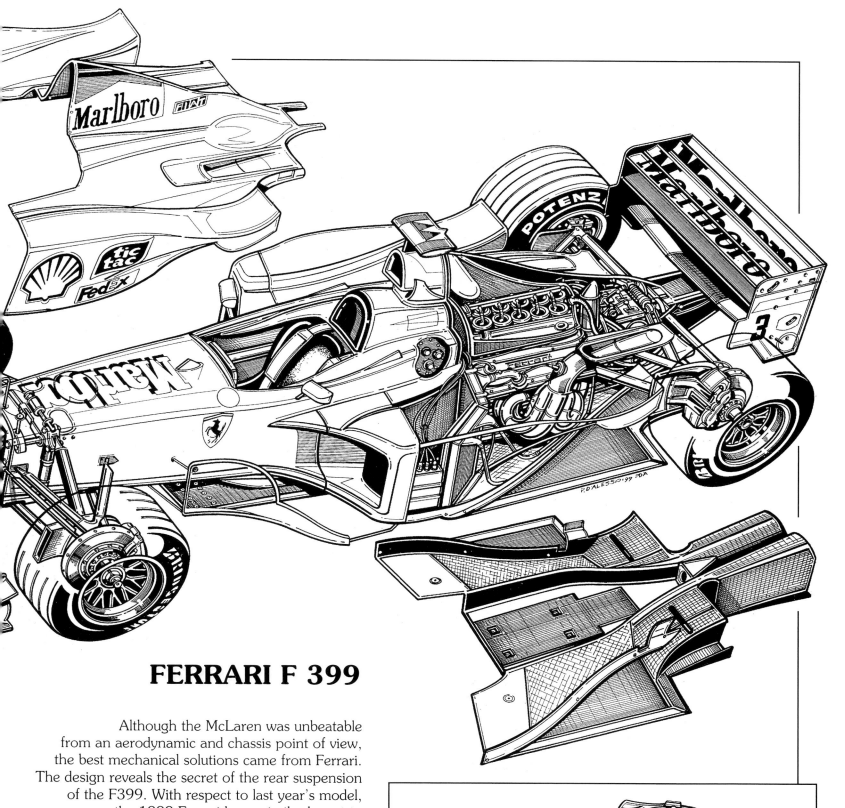

FERRARI F 399

Although the McLaren was unbeatable
from an aerodynamic and chassis point of view,
the best mechanical solutions came from Ferrari.
The design reveals the secret of the rear suspension
of the F399. With respect to last year's model,
the 1999 Ferrari has a similar layout to
the front suspension. It uses inward-slanting
vertical dampers, anchored to the outside
of the transmission, and includes a third horizontal
damper (housed between the two rocker arms),
for control of pitch and roll.
The long, almost horizontal torsion bars
are instead housed inside two specially-made
niches within the carbon-fibre spacer,
which links the titanium gearbox to the engine.
To adjust ride height, all that is required is a simple twist
of a screwdriver in the slit, marked with the sign 'UP',
located immediately behind the mount for
the upper wishbone.

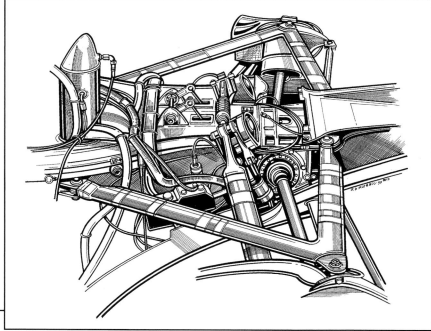

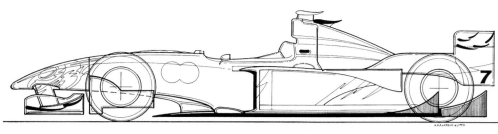

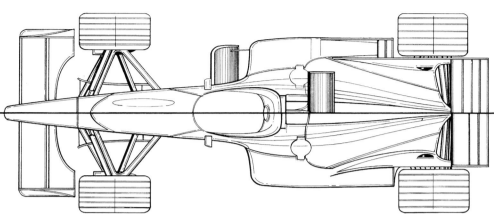

JORDAN 199

If there is one thing that Eddie Jordan can be given credit for, then it's his determination. When the Irish manager debuted his all-green F1 car, designed by former chief mechanic Gary Anderson, in 1991, many thought that it would be another 'flash in the pan' by one of the many adventurers who have tried their hand at Formula 1 in its fifty-year history. Instead, the astute team manager has managed to gradually climb every single step that leads to the top of the F1 pyramid and is now ready to launch an assault on the world title. To reach this peak, Jordan will probably need a lot more time, but this aim is surely within reach for the Anglo-Irish team. After a brilliant 1998, enterprising Eddie's team confirmed itself to be the third force in F1 behind McLaren and Ferrari. What are the car's secrets? On the basis of the results obtained in the last 12 months, there is only one: simplicity. Aware that for the moment he cannot tackle two giants of the calibre of McLaren and Ferrari and that he does not have a sufficiently large budget to do so, Jordan created a professional, but at the same time slim-line outfit and above all asked his designers to produce cars that would not be too difficult to build, run and develop. Damon Hill's and Heinz-Harald Frentzen's 199 was a perfect demonstration of this philosophy. The 1999 Jordan did not contain the aerodynamic perfection achieved by the MP4-14 or the sophisticated mechanical solutions of the F399. It was an extremely reliable car, one that was not particularly refined but on the other hand one without any evident faults. It was designed to stand up to the pressures of a Grand Prix and capitalise on the uncertainties of others whenever necessary. Add to this an engine (the Mugen Honda MF310HD) that was improving rapidly, and you have the reasons for the wins at Magny-Cours and Monza and a superb final few races, which saw the yellow Anglo-Irish cars virtually on the same competitive level as its more victorious rivals.

It is said that the secret of the Jordan 199 lies in its relative simplicity. An example of this can be seen in the front view, where it is possible to note the double upper bulges that house the front suspension dampers. Jordan are the only one of the top teams to have kept this layout, which contains the spring-damper units horizontally in the upper part of the chassis. On the other hand, since last year both McLaren and Ferrari have been using more sophisticated three-way suspension systems with vertical dampers, a third damper for control of pitch and roll and horizontal torsion bars replacing the springs.

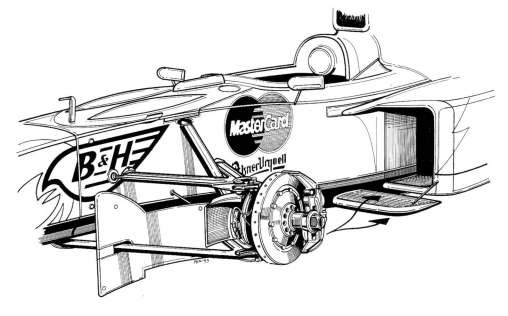

Simplicity however does
not mean that there was no
experimentation on several
new aerodynamic solutions.
In 1999 the Jordan was
the first car to use strange chassis fins
next to the sidepod mounting edge
(also used by Williams afterwards)
to improve air flow and deflect
a certain amount of air to the lower
part of the car. At the Hungarian GP,
the Anglo-Irish team dusted
off the third mid-wing,
mounted just behind the rear
of the air intake.
This aerofoil was particularly
useful on twisty circuits such as
the Hungaroring, where it gave
a valuable increase in downforce.

STEWART SF 3

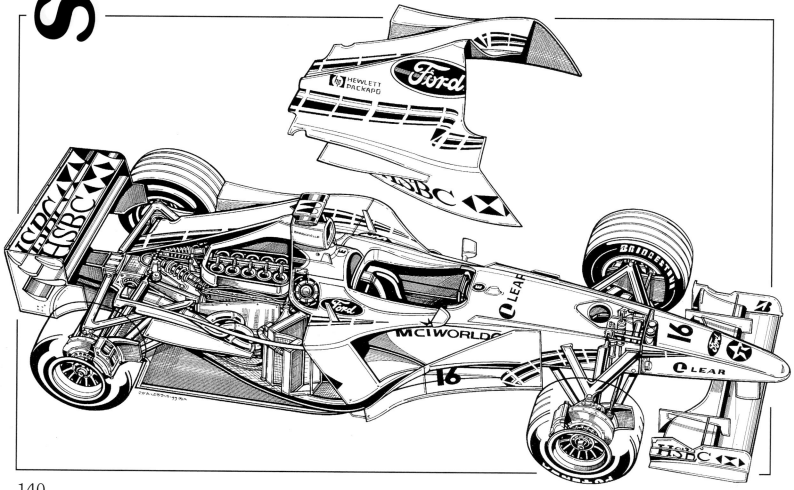

According to Adrian Newey, who knows a thing or two about these matters, the Stewart SF3 ...... was the best copy of the world champion car. The imitation however was not without several interesting developments, starting with the aerodynamics. Alan Jenkins, the father of the SF3, decided not to disown the 1998 project and used the original design of the sidepods. Their layout was different to those of all the other Formula 1 cars: the sides of the '99 Stewart were high and narrow, with the sidepod entry inclined forward. The deflectors in front of the rear wheels are also of a different design. They are almost double the size of their rivals' and their external profile is at a tangent to the outside edge of the flat bottom. Similarities with the McLaren can also be seen in weight distribution (further back also on the Stewart), in the front end (lower, more drooping nose) and in the moving of the steering arm struts to a lower position in order to further lower the car's centre of gravity. All these characteristics however do not explain the incredible step forward made by Stewart in the last few months. The constant presence of Barrichello and Herbert at the front of the field is also due to the greater involvement of Ford in the Formula 1 programme. Starting with the new 10 cylinder CR-1 engine, which is said to be incredible. It is reported to have a similar power output to the Mercedes and, like the German unit, belongs to the latest generation of engines that have remarkably small dimensions and that are right on the weight limit (or even under it).

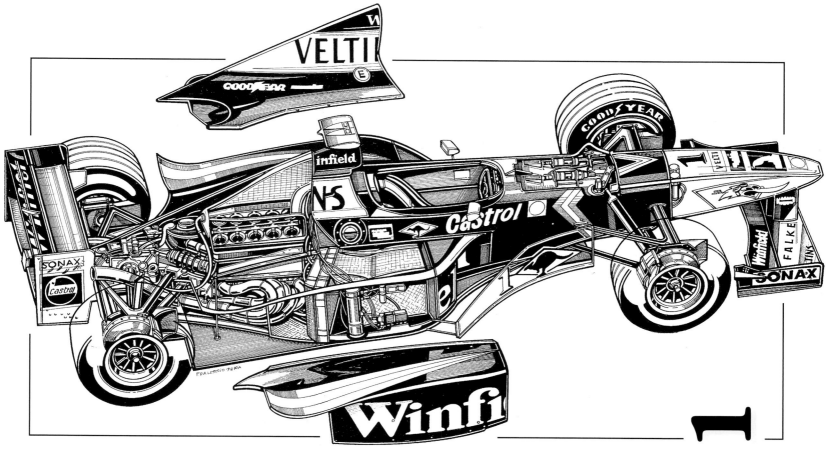

This was the second year
of transition for the team that
dominated the world scene from
1991 to 1997 without a break.
With respect to last year,
the season balance for Williams
was slightly better, especially
if one looks at the second half
of the championship.
After a slow start, the FW21
gradually improved and rightfully
took its place amongst the top
cars behind McLaren.
This recovery demonstrates,
as if there were any need,
that the Grove team has not lost
all of its former glory,
that its designers managed
to recover from the loss
of Adrian Newey and that after
a rather unoriginal transitional
car such as the FW21,

Frank Williams' team is expected
to return to the front in grand style.
Without forgetting that in 2000
the Supertec FB01 will make
way for the new 10 cylinder BMW
factory engine. To get through
this second season of transition,
the engineers led by Patrick Head
basically reverted to the concepts
expressed in the FW20 last year.
Considerable attention was clearly
paid to aerodynamics.
The front of the Williams FW21
underwent the most changes
and the nose was lower,
in accordance with current trends.
Ralf Schumacher's
and Alex Zanardi's cars only
become more competitive
in the second part
of the season after the arrival
of a new rear diffuser.

WILLIAMS FW-21

BENETTON B199

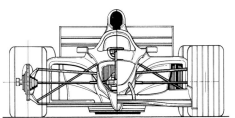

This year's Benetton was not even a pale shadow of the team that dominated the world championship in 1995 with Michael Schumacher. Some people even consider the B199 to be the disappointment of the year. Expectations were high at the start of the year when during the car's launch, Rocco Benetton said he was sure the team would have a great world championship and that they might even score a couple of wins.

Not only did the top rung of the podium remain a mirage for the Enstone team, but even points-scoring finishes were often out of the question for the Fisichella-Wurz pairing. The fault lay with an unpredictable car, crippled by a chronic lack of downforce and in crisis whenever it arrived at slow to medium-fast circuits. Add to this a far from perfect chassis, reliability problems and an engine that was beginning to feel its age, and the result is a portrait of a team that has to be totally revamped. On the eve of the world championship, the Benetton team were banking a lot on the controversial Front Torque Transfer front braking system. According to team engineers, it should have resolved the problem of the wheels locking up during braking, but it didn't and at many races both Fisichella and Wurz preferred not to use it.

PROST AP 02

After a disastrous 1998, Alain Prost must have thought things could not have become any worse. They did get worse however, despite the fact that the team took on, part-time, a designer of the calibre o f John Barnard. Neither Trulli (except for second place in the European GP) nor Panis succeeded in getting amongst the leaders, as they were halted in their attempts by a car that was clearly inferior to the team's expectations and to the cars of their rivals. The reason why is relatively simple to explain. Even though the AP02 was a decisive step forward from the 1998 car, the Prost was a car that was basically just 'old-fashioned'. The fault lay with the Peugeot engine, its size and the need to mount large-sized radiant surfaces, which had a negative influence on the aerodynamic layout of the French blue car. On numerous occasions, the situation was made worse by reliability problems that lost precious world championship points for Alain Prost's team.

SAUBER C 18

Another team that had less success in 1999 than it could have or should have had was Sauber. Unlike other teams, for Sauber the fault for the partial disaster lay solely with the rear of the car. Or to be more exact, the Leo Ress-redesigned transmission which regularly had problems or broke down half-way through the race. With a broken gearbox, a car just cannot go very far. Both Alesi and Diniz then complained about the 10 cylinder Ferrari engine, which was none other than the old 047 from last year and which had not been updated after the first few rounds. As can be seen in the designs, the Sauber C18 only underwent a few detailed revisions from last year's car. Following the trend set by McLaren, the nose was lowered, while the rear maintained the dual fins in front of the rear wheels.

B.A.R. 01

In his declarations at the start of the year, Craig Pollock announced that the BAR team would win races in 1999. Talk comes cheaply however, wins in F1 don't.
The debut of the BAR team in Formula 1 stood out for its series of retirements, an impressive result in a negative sort of way. The chief responsibility lay with the structural fragility of the 01, a car on which everything that could break did break, including delicate elements such as suspension struts or supports and rear wings. From next year however the music will probably change with the arrival of Honda (which has bought 20% of the team) and the new 10 cylinder Japanese engine.

Already rumours are flying around about the potential of the engine, but they may turn out to be less competitive than the semi-official, Mugen/Honda-badged version powering the Jordan.
For BAR's debut in F1, Adrian Reynard designed an extremely neat, but conventional car, that hoped to make reliability one of its strong points. It was a pity therefore that this proved to be the weak link for the 1999 BAR.

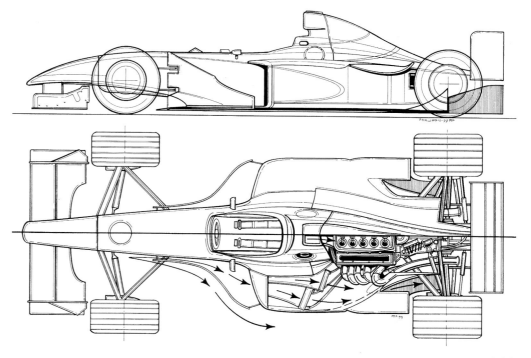

MINARDI M01

Unfortunately once again the team from Emilia-Romagna in Italy propped up the table. This was a real shame because in 1999 Scuderia Minardi tried like never before to shake off this role, producing one of the best cars in its history. But with a limited budget and above all with fragile engines,

it was a miracle they succeeded in picking up one point in the championship. The rear of the M01 was undoubtedly the most successful part of the car from an aerodynamic point of view, and was observed with great attention by more than one rival designer. We would not be surprised if next year some more successful cars make use of an engine cover and side fins similar to those designed by Brunner for the M01.

ARROWS A19

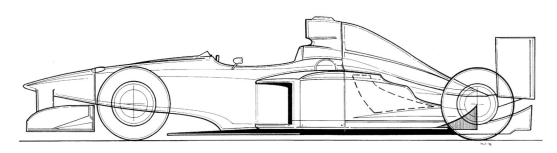

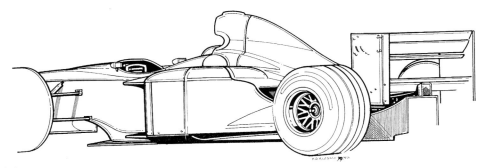

There were two John Barnard-designed cars in circulation: the disappointing Prost AP02 (which the British designer only slightly modified) and the unfortunate Arrows A19, which hit the headlines more for chromatic reasons than anything else. In spite of what the team declared, the car driven by De la Rosa and Takagi was nothing more than last year's car, with a few aerodynamic tweaks at the rear. This was hardly sufficient in a hyper-technological world where modifications came thick and fast at every race, but clearly it was enough to get by throughout the year, in view of the arrival of the 10 cylinder Supertec engine and some munificent sponsor.

146   photo Paolo D'Alessio

148   photo Paolo D'Alessio

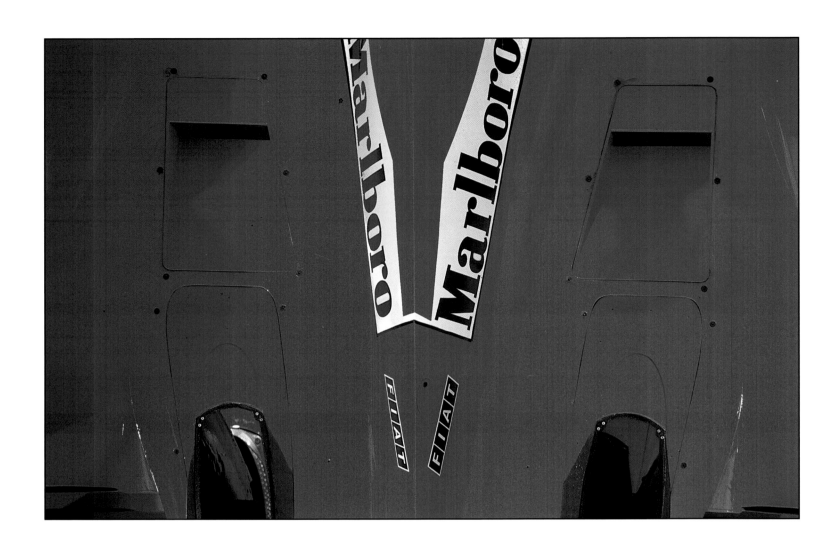

photo Paolo D'Alessio

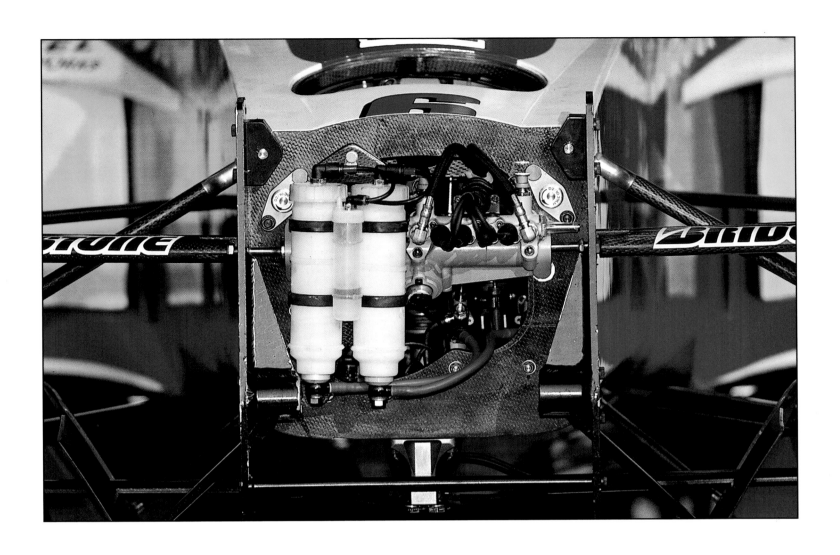

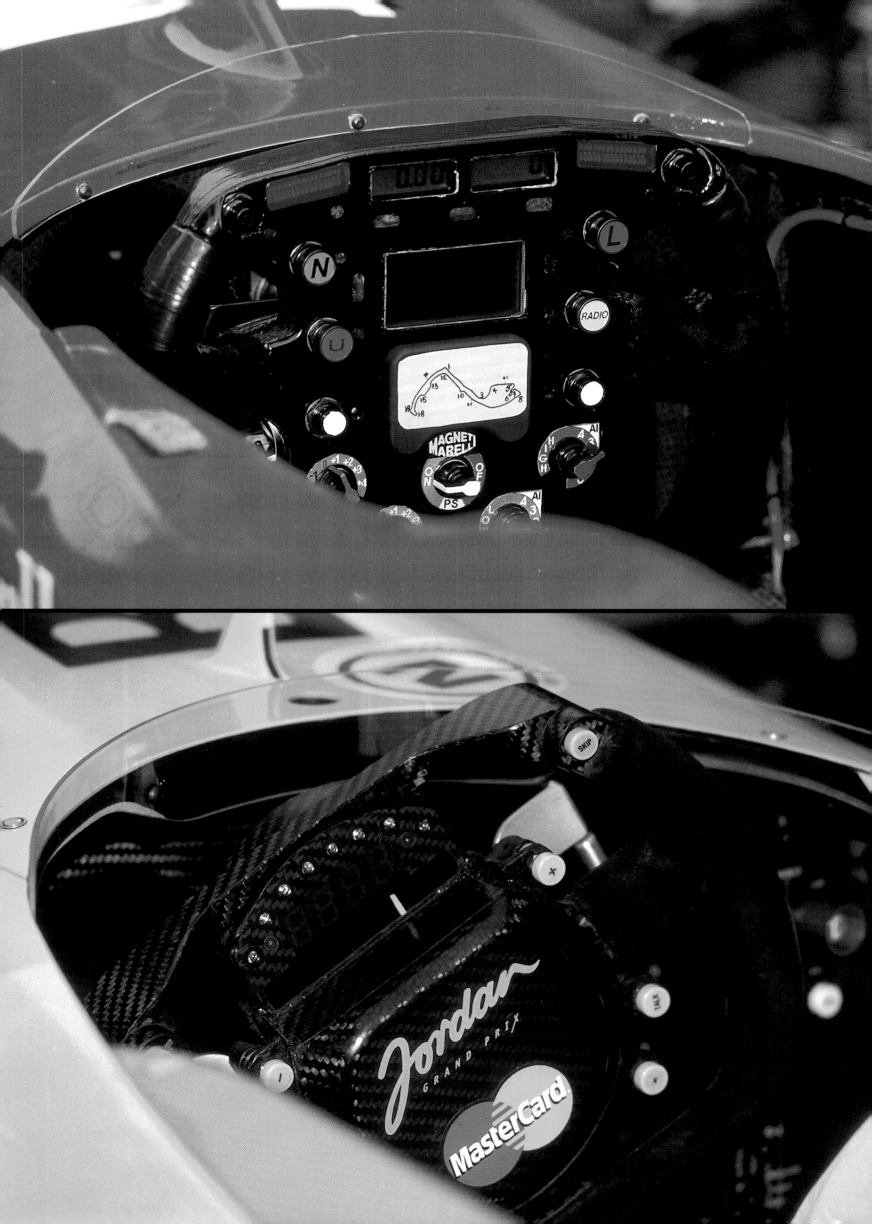

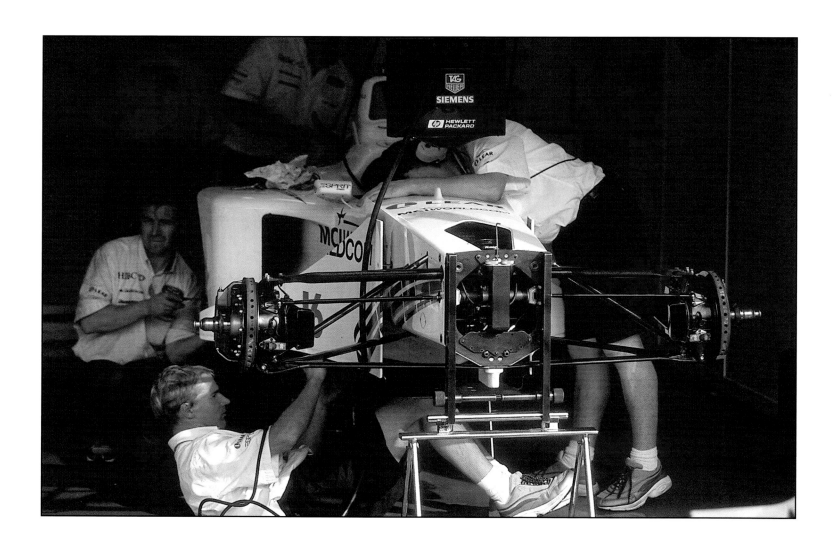

154   photo Paolo D'Alessio

photo Paolo D'Alessio

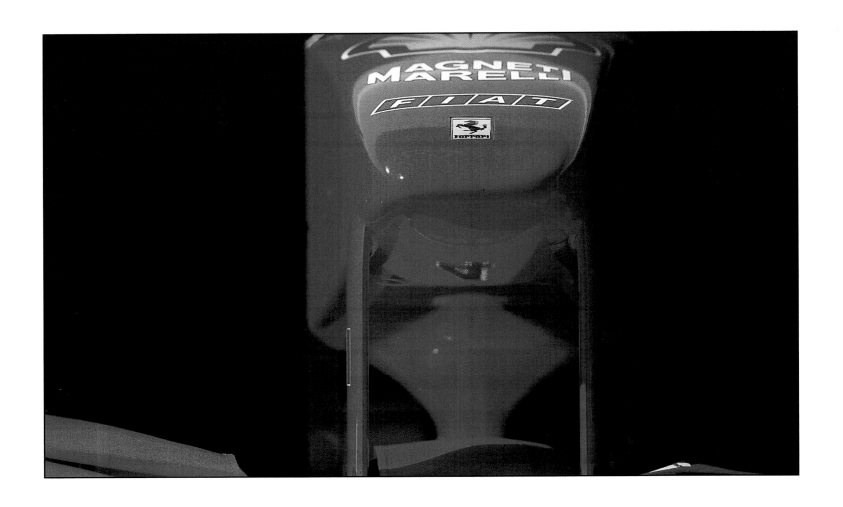

160   photo Paolo D´Alessio

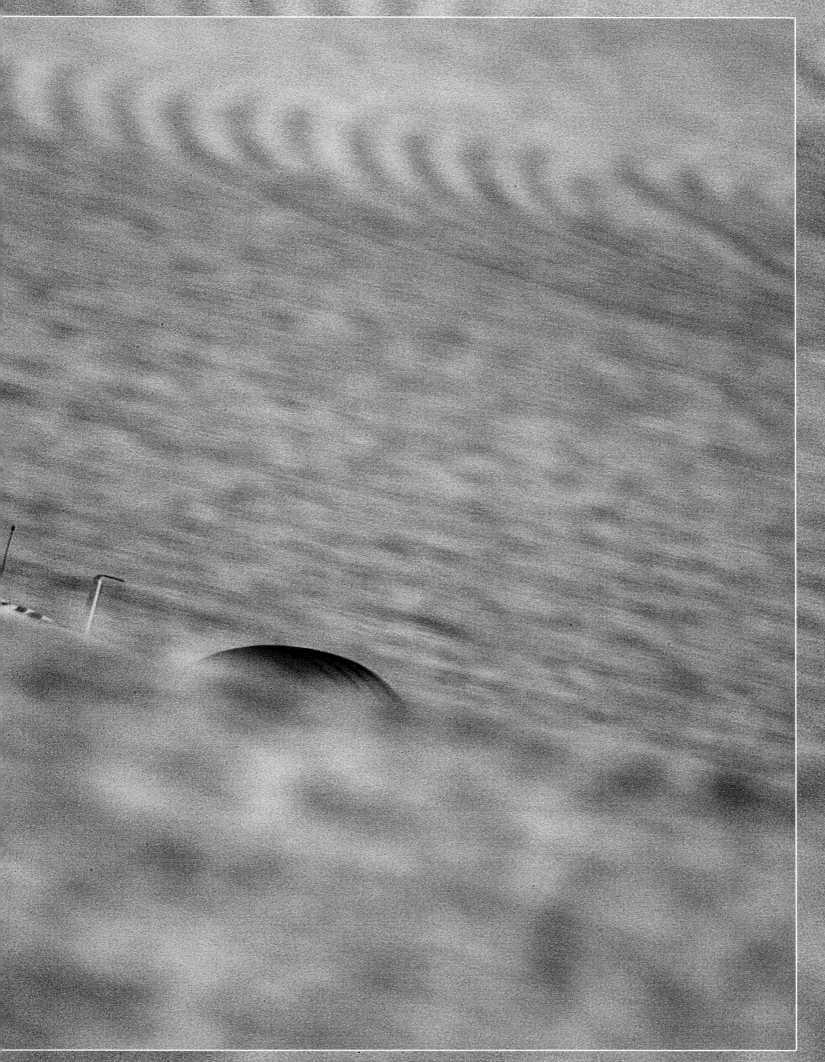

F1
1999

MELBOURNE
MARCH 7

INTERLAGOS
APRIL 11

IMOLA
MAY 2

MONACO
MAY 16

BARCELLONA
MAY 30

MONTREAL
JUNE 13

MAGNY-COURS
JUNE 27

SILVERSTONE
JULY 11

ZELTWEG
JULY 25

HOCKENHEIM
AUGUST 1

HUNGARORING
AUGUST 15

SPA-FRANCORCHAMPS
AUGUST 29

MONZA
SEPTEMBER 12

NÜRBURGRING
SEPTEMBER 26

MALAYSIA
OCTOBER 17

SUZUKA
OCTOBER 31

Mika Hakkinen	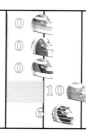											
David Coulthard	0											
Michael Schumacher	0											
Eddie Irvine	10											
Heinz H. Frentzen	6											

The first Grand Prix of the season saw Eddie Irvine's first F1 win after 82 races. For Ferrari, it was the seventh victory in the opening round of the world championship. It was also a sad return to F1 for Alex Zanardi after two triumphant years in the USA. Melbourne saw the debut of Brazil's Ricardo Zonta, and the two Spanish drivers Marc Gené and Pedro De la Rosa. The Austrian driver, Wurz, in his third year with Benetton, captured while picking up a few … tattoos.

	1°	2°	3°
'90	N. Piquet	N. Mansell	A. Prost
'91	A. Senna	N. Mansell	G. Berger
'92	G. Berger	M. Schumacher	M. Brundle
'93	A. Senna	A. Prost	D. Hill
'94	N. Mansell	G. Berger	M. Brundle
'95	D. Hill	O. Panis	G. Morbidelli
'96	D. Hill	J. Villeneuve	E. Irvine
'97	D. Coulthard	M. Schumacher	M. Hakkinen
'98	M. Hakkinen	D. Coulthard	H.H. Frentzen

Australian GP

THE CIRCUIT

7th March 1999 - **Circuit:** Albert Park, Melbourne
Distance: 302,271 KMS - **Spectators:** 120.000

STARTING GRID

M. HAKKINEN McLAREN 1'30"462 (211,037)		**D. COULTHARD** McLAREN 1'30"946 (209,914)
M. SCHUMACHER FERRARI 1'31"781 (208,004)		**R. BARRICHELLO** STEWART 1'32"148 (207,175)
H.H. FRENTZEN JORDAN 1'32"276 (206,888)		**E. IRVINE** FERRARI 1'32"289 (206,859)
G. FISICHELLA BENETTON 1'32"540 (206,298)		**R. SCHUMACHER** WILLIAMS 1'32"691 (205,962)
D. HILL JORDAN 1'32"695 (205,950)		**A. WURZ** BENETTON 1'32"789 (205,744)
J. VILLENEUVE BAR 1'32"888 (205,525)		**J. TRULLI** PROST 1'32"971 (205,341)
J. HERBERT STEWART 1'32"991 (205,297)		**P. DINIZ** SAUBER 1'33"374 (204,455)
A. ZANARDI WILLIAMS 1'33"549 (204,073)		**J. ALESI** SAUBER 1'33"910 (203,288)
T. TAKAGI ARROWS 1'34"182 (202,701)		**P. DE LA ROSA** ARROWS 1'34"244 (202,568)
R. ZONTA BAR 1'34"412 (202,207)		**O. PANIS** PROST 1'35"068 (200,812)
L. BADOER MINARDI 1'35"316 (200,290)		**M. GENE'** MINARDI 1'37"013 (196,786)

They're off! A new year and finally a new face on the top of the winners' podium. Ferrari's Eddie Irvine won the first GP of his career after 81 races, followed home by a rejuvenated, motivated Frentzen (Jordan) and by Schumacher Jr. in a Williams that was an ugly copy of the disappointing '98 car. The two McLarens kicked off the 1999 season in a big way with the first two places on the starting-grid, distancing Schumacher's Ferrari by more than a second and a fantastic Barrichello in the Stewart by almost two. As they were lining up to take their places on the grid, both Stewarts burst into flames with oil leaking onto the exhausts and the start was aborted. The Brazilian started in the spare car from the pit lane, while Schumacher with the Ferrari went to the back of the grid for failing to start on time in the warm-up lap, almost a continuation of a film we had seen before in the last race of '98. Hakkinen's engine also had a few problems on the grid and the mechanics had to move in to resolve them. When the lights finally changed, the two McLarens powered away and led the race until Coulthard got stuck in sixth gear and pitted. In the meantime Villeneuve was flying ... into the wall with a rear wing failure on lap 14. The safety car came out and when it peeled off, Hakkinen put his foot down but found no response due to a throttle linkage problem. Now it was the turn of Irvine to head for victory, while behind the Ulsterman the field was thinning out. Schummy came back into the pits with gear selection problems, restarted again only to lose pieces of his front wing with a puncture, and then stopped for good. Zonta, the young 23 year-old Brazilian introduced to F1 by McLaren and 'on loan' to BAR, was called into the pits twice to check his rear wing. Schumacher Jr. tried to attack Frentzen's second place but he too was losing pieces of bodywork and slowed down to settle for third. Behind the Williams driver came Fisichella and Barrichello in a Stewart that was clearly aiming for better things in 1999.

RESULTS

	DRIVER	CAR	KPH	GAP
1	E. Irvine	Ferrari	190.852	-
2	H.H. Frentzen	Jordan	190.818	1"026
3	R. Schumacher	Williams	190.618	7"012
4	G. Fisichella	Benetton	189.740	33"418
5	R. Barrichello	Stewart	189.038	54"697
6	P. De La Rosa	Arrows	188.071	1'24"316
7	T. Takagi	Arrows	188.007	1'26"288
8	M. Schumacher	Ferrari	187.017	1 lap

RETIREMENTS

DRIVER	CAR	LAP	REASON
J. Alesi	Sauber	0	Gear
D. Hill	Jordan	0	Brakes
J. Villeneuve	BAR	13	Axle-spoiler
D. Coulthard	McLaren	13	Transmission
A. Zanardi	Williams	20	Crashed
M. Hakkinen	McLaren	21	Transmission
O. Panis	Prost	23	Transmission
J. Trulli	Prost	25	Accident
M. Gené	Minardi	25	Accident
P. Diniz	Sauber	27	Transmission
A. Wurz	Benetton	28	Suspension
L. Badoer	Minardi	42	Gear
R. Zonta	BAR	48	Gear

TOPSPEED

DRIVER	MAX.
Hakkinen	295.300
Coulthard	292.500
Irvine	289.800
Hill	289.700
Frentzen	289.600
Barrichello	288.600
Zonta	288.500
Zanardi	288.100
Fisichella	288.000
Schumacher R.	288.000
Schumacher M.	287.300
Wurz	287.100
Herbert	286.700
Diniz	284.800
De La Rosa	283.600
Panis	283.600
Villeneuve	283.500
Alesi	283.200
Badoer	283.000
Trulli	281.900

Mika Hakkinen		10	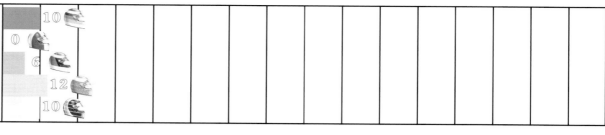												
David Coulthard	0														
Michael Schumacher		6													
Eddie Irvine		12													
Heinz H. Frentzen		10													

After an unhappy start in Australia with transmission problems on both cars, McLaren took revenge in Brazil with its Finnish champion, who set pole position and fastest lap on his way to victory. Stéphane Sarrazin made his debut at the Interlagos circuit. The 25 year-old Frenchman was an official Prost driver but was loaned to Minardi as replacement for Luca Badoer, injured in testing at Fiorano.

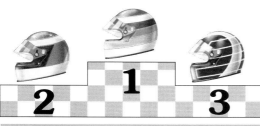

	1°	2°	3°
'90	A. Prost	G. Berger	A. Senna
'91	A. Senna	R. Patrese	G. Berger
'92	N. Mansell	R. Patrese	M. Schumacher
'93	A. Senna	D. Hill	M. Schumacher
'94	M. Schumacher	D. Hill	J. Alesi
'95	G. Berger	M. Hakkinen	J. Alesi
'96	D. Hill	J. Alesi	M. Schumacher
'97	J. Villeneuve	G. Berger	O. Panis
'98	M. Hakkinen	D. Coulthard	M. Schumacher

Brazilian GP

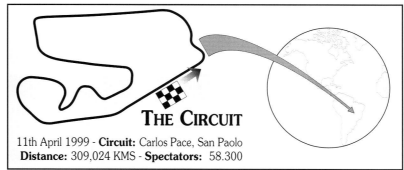

THE CIRCUIT

11th April 1999 - **Circuit:** Carlos Pace, San Paolo
Distance: 309,024 KMS - **Spectators:** 58.300

STARTING GRID

M. HAKKINEN McLaren 1'16"568 (201,797)	**1**	**D. COULTHARD** McLaren 1'16"715 (201,410)	
R. BARRICHELLO Stewart 1'17"305 (199,873)	**2**	**M. SCHUMACHER** Ferrari 1'17"578 (199,170)	
G. FISICHELLA Benetton 1'17"810 (198,576)	**3**	**E. IRVINE** Ferrari 1'17"843 (198,492)	
D. HILL Jordan 1'17"884 (198,387)	**4**	**H.H. FRENTZEN** Jordan 1'17"902 (198,342)	
A. WURZ Benetton 1'18"334 (197,240)	**5**	**J. HERBERT** Stewart 1'18"374 (197,147)	
R. SCHUMACHER Williams 1'18"506 (196,816)	**6**	**O. PANIS** Prost 1'18"636 (196,490)	
J. TRULLI Prost 1'18"684 (196,370)	**7**	**J. ALESI** Sauber 1'18"716 (196,290)	
P. DINIZ Sauber 1'19"194 (195,106)	**8**	**A. ZANARDI** Williams 1'19"452 (194,472)	
S. SARRAZIN Minardi 1'20"016 (193,101)	**9**	**P. DE LA ROSA** Arrows 1'20"076 (192,957)	
T. TAKAGI Arrows 1'20"096 (192,909)	**10**	**M. GENE'** Minardi 1'20"710 (191,441)	
J. VILLENEUVE BAR - (-)	**11**		

R. ZONTA BAR - **NOT QUALIFIED**

The world number 1 was back on the top slot in Brazil but his great rival was just 5 seconds behind him. Even more amazement was aroused by Frentzen, a driver who in '98 seemed to be demotivated or even finished, but who got on the podium in Brazil for the second time in two races. A man who no longer seemed motivated and who in any case was dogged by misfortune was former world champion Damon Hill: in two races he had only managed ten laps and two incidents. Qualifying had confirmed the two McLarens on the front row, followed by an increasingly surprising Barrichello. The Brazilian actually led for a while in the race but retired with engine failure on lap 43 while in third. A new driver made his debut on the circuit dedicated to Carlos Pace: Frenchman Stephane Sarrazin for Minardi, in place of a sidelined Luca Badoer. What a start! Coulthard burned out his clutch on the grid and stalled and the two behind, Fisichella and Schumacher, just managed to avoid him, risking a collision. Mika was powering ahead, followed by Barrichello, but slowed on lap 4 with a gearshift problem and was passed by Barrichello and Schumacher. McLaren panic lasted just a short time because Mika not only managed to hold on to third but also to retake the lead during the pit stops of the two Stewart drivers and the Ferrari. On lap 32, race 'rookie' Sarrazin had a massive shunt at the last corner at more than 270 kph but luckily emerged unhurt. It was time for a Hakkinen pit stop after the Finn had set a series of impressive fastest laps, picking up enough time to ensure he came out of the pits ahead of Schummy. Barrichello said goodbye to an excellent third place, which went to the consistent Frentzen. The German ran out of fuel on the last lap, but was safe thanks to his lead over Schumacher Jr. in fourth place and again in the points.

RESULTS

	DRIVER	CAR	KPH	GAP
1	M. Hakkinen	McLaren	192.994	-
2	M. Schumacher	Ferrari	192.829	4"925
3	H.H. Frentzen	Jordan	190.542	1 lap
4	R. Schumacher	Williams	189.685	1 lap
5	E. Irvine	Ferrari	189.677	1 lap
6	O. Panis	Prost	188.043	1 lap
7	A. Wurz	Benetton	187.365	2 laps
8	T. Takagi	Arrows	184.750	3 laps
9	M. Gené	Minardi	183.099	3 laps

RETIREMENTS

DRIVER	CAR	LAP	REASON
D. Hill	Jordan	10	Accident
J. Herbert	Stewart	16	Hydraulic circuit
J. Trulli	Prost	21	Gear
D. Coulthard	McLaren	22	Gear
J. Alesi	Sauber	27	Gear
S. Sarrazin	Minardi	31	Accident
G. Fisichella	Benetton	38	Clutch
P. Diniz	Sauber	42	Accident
R. Barrichello	Stewart	42	Engine
A. Zanardi	Williams	43	Gear
J. Villeneuve	BAR	48	Hydraulic circuit
P. De La Rosa	Arrows	52	Hydraulic circuit

TOPSPEED

DRIVER	MAX.
Hakkinen	311.600
Herbert	309.500
Coulthard	309.200
Alesi	309.200
M. Schumacher	307.600
Hill	303.500
Panis	303.200
Frentzen	302.500
Wurz	301.900
Fisichella	301.600
Irvine	301.500
Trulli	301.300
Villeneuve	301.200
Takagi	301.000
Barrichello	301.000
Sarrazin	300.500
R. Schumacher	299.700
De La Rosa	297.900
Diniz	297.600
Zanardi	297.000

Mika Hakkinen	10 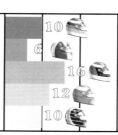											
David Coulthard	6											
Michael Schumacher	16											
Eddie Irvine	12											
Heinz H. Frentzen	10											

The Brazilian from San Paolo, Rubens Barrichello, took his Stewart onto the podium at Imola. With 99 F1 races to his name, Rubens made his debut in 1993 in South Africa with a Jordan-Hart. But to the joy of the thousands of Italian tifosi, the top rung of the podium went to Michael Schumacher, who took over the lead of the race after Hakkinen went off in front of the pits straight after overtaking Coulthard thanks to brilliant pit-stop strategy by Ross Brawn.

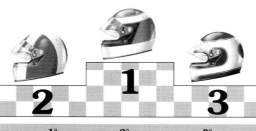

	1°	2°	3°
'90	R. Patrese	G. Berger	A. Nannini
'91	A. Senna	G. Berger	J. Lehto
'92	N. Mansell	R. Patrese	A. Senna
'93	A. Prost	M. Schumacher	M. Brundell
'94	M. Schumacher	N. Larini	M. Hakkinen
'95	D. Hill	J. Alesi	G. Berger
'96	D. Hill	M. Schumacher	G. Berger
'97	H.H. Frentzen	M. Schumacher	E. Irvine
'98	D. Coulthard	M. Schumacher	E. Irvine

San Marino GP

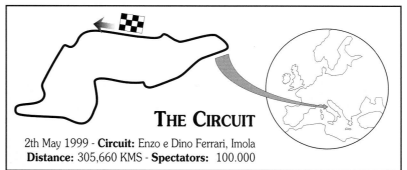

THE CIRCUIT

2th May 1999 - **Circuit:** Enzo e Dino Ferrari, Imola
Distance: 305,660 KMS - **Spectators:** 100.000

STARTING GRID

M. HAKKINEN McLAREN 1'26"362 (205,507)		D. COULTHARD McLAREN 1'26"384 (205,455)	**1**
M. SCHUMACHER FERRARI 1'26"538 (205,089)		E. IRVINE FERRARI 1'26"993 (204,016)	**2**
J. VILLENEUVE BAR 1'27"313 (203,269)		R. BARRICHELLO STEWART 1'27"409 (203,045)	**3**
H.H. FRENTZEN JORDAN 1'27"613 (202,573)		D. HILL JORDAN 1'27"708 (202,353)	**4**
R. SCHUMACHER WILLIAMS 1'27"770 (202,210)		A. ZANARDI WILLIAMS 1'28"142 (201,357)	**5**
O. PANIS PROST 1'28"205 (201,213)		J. HERBERT STEWART 1'28"246 (201,120)	**6**
J. ALESI SAUBER 1'28"253 (201,104)		J. TRULLI PROST 1'28"403 (200,762)	**7**
P. DINIZ SAUBER 1'28"599 (200,318)		G. FISICHELLA BENETTON 1'28"750 (199,977)	**8**
A. WURZ BENETTON 1'28"765 (199,944)		P. DE LA ROSA ARROWS 1'29"293 (198,761)	**9**
M. SALO BAR 1'29"451 (198,410)		T. TAKAGI ARROWS 1'29"656 (197,957)	**10**
M. GENE' MINARDI 1'30"035 (197,123)		L. BADOER MINARDI 1'30"945 (195,151)	**11**

When Formula 1 returned to Europe and to the Imola circuit dedicated to Enzo and Dino Ferrari, once again the scarlet cars managed to send wild more than 100,000 tifosi in the stands and the Tosa curve that has virtually become the symbol of the circuit. Qualifying however was the same old story: two McLarens ahead of two Ferraris. Behind finally we saw a determined Villeneuve and the usual Barrichello. Schumacher's win was a cocktail of driver ability, car performance, pit strategy and fantastic work by the mechanics. The start again left the spectators with bated breath. Villeneuve was left stranded and a 'guardian angel' somewhere was on hand to prevent a tragedy from happening, as the rest of the field avoided the Canadian. Hakkinen took the lead and set a cracking pace. The Finn was almost 2" ahead first time round and lapped Gene on lap 17, but just as he was exiting the last corner, he got it all wrong, went on the kerb and pitched his McLaren into the wall.

Driver error? Electronics? Whatever it was, the tifosi went wild and this gave a further push to Schumacher, lying second behind Coulthard. Now it was time for a bit of Ferrari strategy, as Schummy came in for a quick 6.5" pit stop. That was the turning-point of the race. With less fuel on board, Schummy began a series of record laps, pulling out such a big lead over Coulthard that he could afford to make a second rapid stop to take on the fuel he needed to complete the race. The red flags were waving as the Ferrari no.3 came past the wall where all the mechanics were celebrating his victory. Behind the German, Coulthard took second place followed by Barrichello, who was finally able to prove his worth without an engine failure. Fourth place went to Damon Hill, who saw the chequered flag for the first time this year, fifth to Fisichella and sixth to one of the tifosi's idols, Jean Alesi with the Sauber. This was an important point for the Swiss manufacturer, which had seen its two cars retire in both the previous races.

RESULTS

	DRIVER	CAR	KPH	GAP
1	M. Schumacher	Ferrari	195.481	-
2	D. Coulthard	McLaren	195.333	4"265
3	R. Barrichello	Stewart	192.259	1 lap
4	D. Hill	Jordan	192.228	1 lap
5	G. Fisichella	Benetton	190.893	1 lap
6	J. Alesi	Sauber	190.689	1 lap
7	M. Salo	BAR	189.268	3 laps
8	L. Badoer	Minardi	185.732	3 laps
9	M. Gené	Minardi	184.985	3 laps
10	J. Herbert	Stewart	191.264	4 laps
11	A. Zanardi	Williams	191.001	4 laps

RETIREMENTS

DRIVER	CAR	LAP	REASON
J. Trulli	Prost	0	Accident
J. Villeneuve	BAR	0	Gear
A. Wurz	Benetton	5	Accident
P. De La Rosa	Arrows	5	Accident
M. Hakkinen	McLaren	17	Accident
R. Schumacher	Williams	28	Engine
T. Takagi	Arrows	29	Engine
H.H. Frentzen	Jordan	46	Accident
E. Irvine	Ferrari	46	Engine
O. Panis	Prost	48	Engine
P. Diniz	Sauber	49	Accident

TOPSPEED

DRIVER	MAX.
Hakkinen	303.200
Coulthard	302.100
Frentzen	299.800
M. Schumacher	299.000
Irvine	298.000
Barrichello	297.100
Alesi	295.600
Panis	295.000
Herbert	294.900
Hill	294.100
Diniz	293.000
Fisichella	293.000
De La Rosa	293.000
Villeneuve	291.800
Takagi	290.900
R. Schumacher	290.600
Trulli	290.200
Zanardi	290.200
Wurz	289.900
Salo	289.600

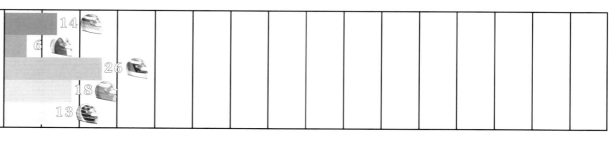

Italians in seventh heaven! With its number 1 driver, Ferrari repeated the Imola win and pulled off an extraordinary victory at Montecarlo. Irvine also finished runner-up in the second Ferrari. With this win, his sixteenth in a Ferrari, Schumacher became the Prancing Horse's most successful driver, overtaking Lauda on 15 victories. Mika Salo again stood in for the injured Zonta in the BAR, as at Imola. The Finnish driver had an unfortunate race however, crashing into the guard-rail at the Loews corner after just 8 laps.

	1°	2°	3°
'90	A. Senna	J. Alesi	G. Berger
'91	A. Senna	N. Mansell	J. Alesi
'92	A. Senna	N. Mansell	R. Patrese
'93	A. Senna	D. Hill	J. Alesi
'94	M. Schumacher	M. Brundle	G. Berger
'95	M. Schumacher	D. Hill	G. Berger
'96	O. Panis	D. Coulthard	J. Herbert
'97	M. Schumacher	R. Barrichello	E. Irvine
'98	M. Hakkinen	G. Fisichella	E. Irvine

Monaco GP

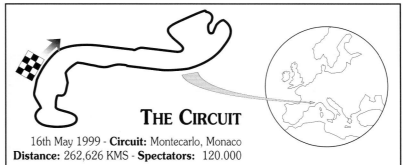

THE CIRCUIT

16th May 1999 - **Circuit:** Montecarlo, Monaco
Distance: 262,626 KMS - **Spectators:** 120.000

STARTING GRID

M. HAKKINEN McLAREN
1'20"547 (150,486)
(1)

M. SCHUMACHER FERRARI
1'20"611 (150,367)

D. COULTHARD McLAREN
1'20"956 (149,726)
(2)

E. IRVINE FERRARI
1'21"011 (149,624)

R. BARRICHELLO STEWART
1'21"530 (148,672)
(3)

H.H. FRENTZEN JORDAN
1'21"556 (148,624)

J. TRULLI PROST
1'21"769 (148,237)
(4)

J. VILLENEUVE BAR
1'21"827 (148,132)

G. FISICHELLA BENETTON
1'21"938 (147,931)
(5)

A. WURZ BENETTON
1'21"968 (147,877)

A. ZANARDI WILLIAMS
1'22"152 (147,546)
(6)

M. SALO BAR
1'22"241 (147,386)

J. HERBERT STEWART
1'22"248 (147,374)
(7)

J. ALESI SAUBER
1'22"354 (147,184)

P. DINIZ SAUBER
1'22"659 (146,641)
(8)

R. SCHUMACHER WILLIAMS
1'22"719 (146,535)

D. HILL JORDAN
1'22"832 (146,335)
(9)

O. PANIS PROST
1'22"916 (146,187)

T. TAKAGI ARROWS
1'23"290 (145,530)
(10)

L. BADOER MINARDI
1'23"765 (144,705)

P. DE LA ROSA ARROWS
1'24"260 (143,855)
(11)

M. GENE' MINARDI
1'24"914 (142,747)

Ferrari first and second at the flag, as stipulated in the contract (Irvine's), with Mika's McLaren on the bottom rung of the podium and Frentzen in the points once again, to the joy of Eddie Jordan who saw the value of his team (as well as his wallet) rocket sky-high in Montecarlo. Damon Hill went out in an incident on lap 4 and Coulthard retired with gearbox problems half-way through the race.
It was Schumacher's fourth victory on the street circuit, a victory that was never in doubt. He led the race from lap 1 to 78 after dominating qualifying, with the exception of Hakkinen's successful last-ditch attempt at pole. At the start Schummy blasted away from the McLaren and shut the door on Mika at the first corner.
As always, the Monaco circuit was a total wipe-out for engines, gearboxes and suspensions. Badoer came to a halt with gearbox failure on the 10th lap, Gené hit the tyre wall at Ste Devote on his 25th lap, then Villeneuve went straight on at the chicane on a fluid leak from his own BAR.
Behind Schumacher in the lead, virtually the only battle was between Hakkinen and Irvine. At the Finn's pit-stop, Irvine took over 2nd place and held on until the end despite pitting for a second rapid stop and despite Mika's record lap at the end of the race in a desperate attempt to catch the Ulsterman.

RESULTS

	DRIVER	CAR	KPH	GAP
1	M. Schumacher	Ferrari	143.864	-
2	E. Irvine	Ferrari	143.200	30"476
3	M. Hakkinen	McLaren	143.049	37"483
4	H.H. Frentzen	Jordan	142.692	54"009
5	G. Fisichella	Benetton	142.001	1 lap
6	A. Wurz	Benetton	141.675	1 lap
7	J. Trulli	Prost	141.288	1 lap
8	A. Zanardi	Williams	139.799	2 laps
9	R. Barrichello	Stewart	142.067	7 laps

RETIREMENTS

DRIVER	CAR	LAP	REASON
D. Hill	Jordan	3	Accident
L. Badoer	Minardi	10	Gear
M. Gené	Minardi	24	Accident
P. De La Rosa	Arrows	30	Gear
J. Herbert	Stewart	32	Suspension
J. Villeneuve	BAR	32	Accident
T. Takagi	Arrows	36	Engine
M. Salo	BAR	36	Accident
D. Coulthard	McLaren	36	Gear
O. Panis	Prost	40	Accident
P. Diniz	Sauber	49	Accident
J. Alesi	Sauber	50	Suspension
R. Schumacher	Williams	54	Accident

TOPSPEED

DRIVER	MAX.
Coulthard	288.000
Hakkinen	284.400
M. Schumacher	284.200
Herbert	282.100
Hill	281.900
Barrichello	281.500
R. Schumacher	281.300
Zanardi	280.800
Fisichella	280.200
Frentzen	280.000
Villeneuve	280.000
Irvine	279.500
Alesi	279.200
Panis	279.000
Diniz	278.900
Salo	278.900
De La Rosa	278.900
Wurz	278.400
Badoer	277.700
Trulli	276.400

Mika Hakkinen															
David Coulthard															
Michael Schumacher															
Eddie Irvine															
Heinz H. Frentzen															

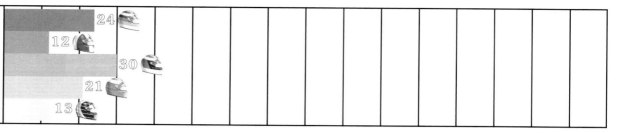

The opening photo is dedicated to Jacques Villeneuve, finally in a good grid position (6th), who got off to a fantastic start. At the end of lap 1, Jacques was third behind the two McLarens after slipping past the two Ferraris at the first curve. For 23 laps Schummy had to follow the Canadian BAR driver. Instead Gené with the Minardi (gearbox failure) and Panis with the Post (stalled engine) were not so fortunate.

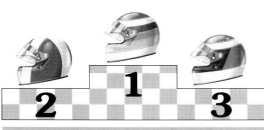

	1°	2°	3°
'90	A. Prost	N. Mansell	A. Nannini
'91	N. Mansell	A. Prost	R. Patrese
'92	N. Mansell	M. Schumacher	J. Alesi
'93	A. Prost	A. Senna	M. Schumacher
'94	D. Hill	M. Schumacher	M. Brundell
'95	M. Schumacher	J. Herbert	G. Berger
'96	M. Schumacher	J. Alesi	J. Villeneuve
'97	J. Villeneuve	O. Panis	J. Alesi
'98	M. Hakkinen	D. Coulthard	M. Schumacher

Spanish GP

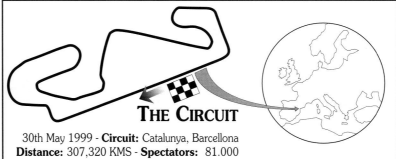

THE CIRCUIT

30th May 1999 - **Circuit:** Catalunya, Barcellona
Distance: 307,320 KMS - **Spectators:** 81.000

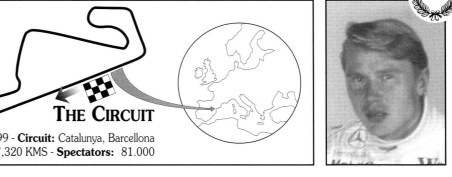

STARTING GRID

M. HAKKINEN McLAREN
1'22"088 (207,348)
(1)

E. IRVINE FERRARI
1'22"219 (207,018)

D. COULTHARD McLAREN
1'22"244 (206,955)
(2)

M. SCHUMACHER FERRARI
1'22"277 (206,872)

J. ALESI SAUBER
1'22"388 (206,593)
(3)

J. VILLENEUVE BAR
1'22"703 (205,806)

R. BARRICHELLO STEWART
1'22"920 (205,268)
(4)

H.H. FRENTZEN JORDAN
1'22"938 (205,223)

J. TRULLI PROST
1'23"194 (204,592)
(5)

R. SCHUMACHER WILLIAMS
1'23"303 (204,324)

D. HILL JORDAN
1'23"317 (204,290)
(6)

P. DINIZ SAUBER
1'23"331 (204,255)

G. FISICHELLA BENETTON
1'23"333 (204,250)
(7)

J. HERBERT STEWART
1'23"505 (203,830)

O. PANIS PROST
1'23"559 (203,698)
(8)

M. SALO BAR
1'23"683 (203,396)

A. ZANARDI WILLIAMS
1'23"703 (203,348)
(9)

A. WURZ BENETTON
1'23"824 (203,054)

P. DE LA ROSA ARROWS
1'24"619 (201,146)
(10)

T. TAKAGI ARROWS
1'25"280 (199,587)

M. GENE' MINARDI
1'25"672 (198,674)
(11)

L. BADOER MINARDI
1'25"833 (198,301)

Things were looking good for Ferrari after Monaco. Two cars in the first two places and Hakkinen 12 points behind Schummy. Nevertheless in Spain it was McLaren who scored a 'double-whammy', repeating the 1998 result and demonstrating that the Spanish circuit is favourable for the Anglo-German cars. Mika set pole and won easily, leading almost the entire 65 laps race. Coulthard also had no problems holding on to second place from lights to flag while Schumacher, who found himself behind Villeneuve at the start, encountered major difficulties in overtaking him and could only manage it on lap 24 when they both went in for a pit-stop. Once free of Villeneuve,

Schumacher began to notch up a series of fastest laps that reduced the gap between him and Coulthard to 3 seconds. In the meantime, Villeneuve came into the pits for the second time and the traditional professional pit-stop turned into a sort of farce, with the mechanics holding on to the damaged rear wing trying to rip off the upper spoiler. The scene continued for a few seconds but the wing refused to budge. Finally Jacques tried to get going again but the transmission failed as he pulled away, and the Canadian was out. Back down the field Trulli was defending sixth place (first points of 1999) from Damon Hill, who had passed Barrichello for seventh in what was virtually the only such manoeuvre of the race.

RESULTS

	DRIVER	CAR	KPH	GAP
1	M. Hakkinen	McLaren	195.608	-
2	D. Coulthard	McLaren	195.393	6"238
3	M. Schumacher	Ferrari	195.234	10"845
4	E. Irvine	Ferrari	194.569	30"182
5	R. Schumacher	Williams	192.637	1'27"208
6	J. Trulli	Prost	192.245	1 lap
7	D. Hill	Jordan	192.211	1 lap
8	R. Barrichello	Stewart	192.147	1 lap
9	M. Salo	BAR	190.329	1 lap
10	G. Fisichella	Benetton	190.274	1 lap
11	A. Wurz	Benetton	190.047	1 lap
12	P. De La Rosa	Arrows	188.666	2 laps
13	T. Takagi	Arrows	185.746	3 laps

RETIREMENTS

DRIVER	CAR	LAP	REASON
M. Gené	Minardi	0	Gear
O. Panis	Prost	24	Oil pressure
A. Zanardi	Williams	24	Gear
J. Alesi	Sauber	27	Gear
H.H. Frentzen	Jordan	35	Axle-shaft
J. Herbert	Stewart	40	Transmission
P. Diniz	Sauber	40	Gear
J. Villeneuve	BAR	40	Gear
L. Badoer	Minardi	50	Spun off

TOPSPEED

DRIVER	MAX.
Hakkinen	320.700
Coulthard	318.300
Trulli	312.200
Hill	312.000
Barrichello	312.000
Villeneuve	310.700
R. Schumacher	309.400
Panis	308.900
Salo	308.300
Herbert	307.900
Frentzen	307.700
M. Schumacher	307.400
Alesi	307.200
Fisichella	306.200
Irvine	305.800
Diniz	305.100
De La Rosa	304.900
Wurz	304.000
Zanardi	303.800
Takagi	301.700

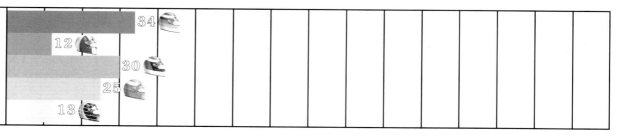
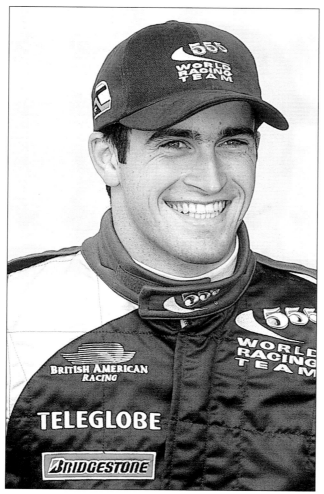

A smiling Ricardo Zonta (above) before the start of the Canadian GP. His smile would not last very long because he crashed into the wall after just two laps. Not to be outdone, team leader Villeneuve imitated him at the same point 33 laps later. Hill on lap 16 and Schumacher on lap 29 (when he was in the lead of the race) did exactly the same thing at the same wall. Champagne therefore for Hakkinen, who turned in a faultless performance.

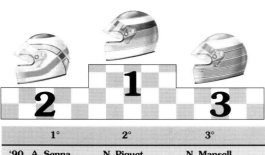

Canadian GP

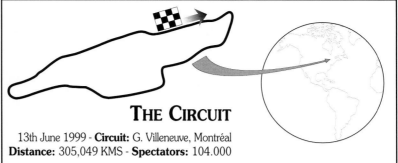

THE CIRCUIT

13th June 1999 - **Circuit:** G. Villeneuve, Montréal
Distance: 305,049 KMS - **Spectators:** 104.000

	1°	2°	3°
'90	A. Senna	N. Piquet	N. Mansell
'91	N. Piquet	S. Modena	R. Patrese
'92	G. Berger	M. Schumacher	J. Alesi
'93	A. Prost	M. Schumacher	D. Hill
'94	M. Schumacher	D. Hill	J. Alesi
'95	J. Alesi	R. Barrichello	E. Irvine
'96	D. Hill	J. Villeneuve	J. Alesi
'97	M. Schumacher	J. Alesi	G. Fisichella
'98	M. Schumacher	G. Fisichella	E. Irvine

STARTING GRID

M. SCHUMACHER FERRARI
1'19"298 (200,706)

M. HAKKINEN McLAREN
1'19"327 (200,633)

(1)

E. IRVINE FERRARI
1'19"440 (200,347)

D. COULTHARD McLAREN
1'19"729 (199,621)

(2)

R. BARRICHELLO STEWART
1'19"930 (199,119)

H.H. FRENTZEN JORDAN
1'20"158 (198,553)

(3)

G. FISICHELLA BENETTON
1'20"378 (198,009)

J. ALESI SAUBER
1'20"459 (197,810)

(4)

J. TRULLI PROST
1'20"557 (197,569)

J. HERBERT STEWART
1'20"829 (196,905)

(5)

A. WURZ BENETTON
1'21"000 (196,489)

A. ZANARDI WILLIAMS
1'21"076 (196,305)

(6)

R. SCHUMACHER WILLIAMS
1'21"081 (196,293)

D. HILL JORDAN
1'21"094 (196,261)

(7)

O. PANIS PROST
1'21"252 (195,879)

J. VILLENEUVE BAR
1'21"302 (195,759)

(8)

R. ZONTA BAR
1'21"467 (195,363)

P. DINIZ SAUBER
1'21"571 (195,113)

(9)

T. TAKAGI ARROWS
1'21"693 (194,822)

P. DE LA ROSA ARROWS
1'22"613 (192,652)

(10)

L. BADOER MINARDI
1'22"808 (192,199)

M. GENE' MINARDI
1'23"387 (190,864)

(11)

The Circuit Gilles Villeneuve is favourable to Ferrari and this was therefore an opportunity not to be missed to bring Hakkinen's charge to an end after his win in Spain. It was with this spirit that the Prancing Horse team arrived in Montreal at the start of June. Their optimism was confirmed during qualifying, with Schumacher's first pole position of the year, and at the start when the Ferrari driver took the lead and defended his position from an aggressive Hakkinen at the first curve. But not even one lap was completed before the safety car came out due to an incident caused by Trulli who bounced into Alesi and Barrichello. Alesi was out while Barrichello continued the race but his Stewart had damaged steering and he withdrew on lap 14. While Schumacher was continuing in the lead, all sorts of things were happening behind. Riccardo Zonta (BAR) crashed into the wall at the first restart, followed shortly after by Hill at the same point on lap 16. Schumacher's Ferrari was circulating like a Swiss watch. Maybe even too aggressively, setting numerous fastest laps ... until lap 29, when he lost grip exiting the final corner and crashed into the wall. This was an unforgivable mistake and let McLaren through into the lead until the chequered flag. After Schummy, another world champion - Villeneuve - also crashed at the same point. With Mika safely in the lead, the battle began in earnest between Coulthard and Irvine, with late braking, a spot of grass-cutting and shortcuts through the chicane. Irvine, who set the first fastest lap of his career, was like a man possessed and after Coulthard, also passed Herbert and R.Schumacher for third place. Fisichella and Frentzen disputed second place which went to the Italian when brake disc failure pitched Frentzen off the track with three laps to go. It was a nasty incident and the German emerged from the car clearly in a state of shock.

RESULTS

	DRIVER	CAR	KPH	GAP
1	M. Hakkinen	McLaren	180.155	-
2	G. Fisichella	Benetton	180.132	0"781
3	E. Irvine	Ferrari	180.102	1"796
4	R. Schumacher	Williams	180.084	2"391
5	J. Herbert	Stewart	180.072	2"804
6	P. Diniz	Sauber	180.045	3"710
7	D. Coultrard	McLaren	180.007	5"003
8	M. Gené	Minardi	177.422	1 lap
9	O. Panis	Prost	177.400	1 lap
10	L. Badoer	Minardi	174.866	2 laps
11	H.H. Frentzen	Jordan	181.787	4 laps

RETIREMENTS

DRIVER	CAR	LAP	REASON
A. Wurz	Benetton	0	Axle-shaft
J. Trulli	Prost	0	Accident
J. Alesi	Sauber	0	Accident
R. Zonta	BAR	2	Accident
R. Barrichello	Stewart	14	Retirement
D. Hill	Jordan	14	Accident
P. De La Rosa	Arrows	22	Transmission
M. Schumacher	Ferrari	29	Accident
J. Villeneuve	BAR	34	Accident
T. Takagi	Arrows	41	Transmission
A. Zanardi	Williams	50	Brakes

TOPSPEED

DRIVER	MAX.
Coulthard	324.700
Trulli	321.400
M. Schumacher	320.900
Frentzen	320.300
Hill	320.300
Takagi	320.300
Hakkinen	320.000
Herbert	319.900
Wurz	319.700
Barrichello	319.600
Irvine	319.400
De La Rosa	319.100
Panis	318.700
Zonta	316.100
Diniz	315.300
Alesi	315.100
Fisichella	314.000
Badoer	313.700
Gené	313.300
Zanardi	313.000

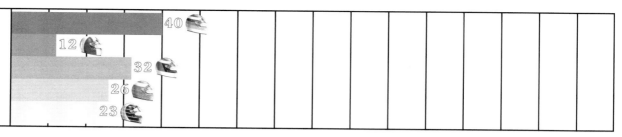

Question: Who set the fastest lap in the race? Answer: Oliver Gavin in the Mercedes Safety Car. Only joking of course, but behind him Zonta, Fisichella, Villeneuve and Wurz all spun off, while Gené even crashed out. Barrichello (third at the finish) celebrated pole position after qualifying. For the record, it was his second ever pole in 104 GPs. On the podium, Frentzen celebrated his second career win with Eddie Irvine.

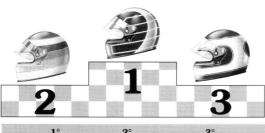

	1°	2°	3°
'90	A. Prost	I. Capelli	A. Senna
'91	N. Mansell	A. Prost	A. Senna
'92	N. Mansell	A. Prost	M. Brundle
'93	A. Prost	D. Hill	M. Schumacher
'94	M. Schumacher	D. Hill	G. Berger
'95	M. Schumacher	D. Hill	D. Coulthard
'96	D. Hill	J. Villeneuve	J. Alesi
'97	M. Schumacher	H.H. Frentzen	E. Irvine
'98	M. Schumacher	E. Irvine	M. Hakkinen

French GP

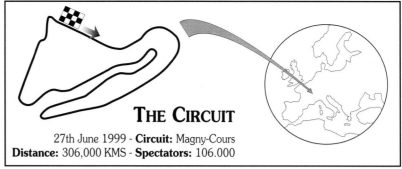

THE CIRCUIT

27th June 1999 - **Circuit:** Magny-Cours
Distance: 306,000 KMS - **Spectators:** 106.000

STARTING GRID

1
R. BARRICHELLO STEWART
1'38"441 (155,423)
J. ALESI SAUBER
1'38"881 (154,731)

2
O. PANIS PROST
1'40"400 (152,390)
D. COULTHARD MCLAREN
1'40"403 (152,386)

3
H.H. FRENTZEN JORDAN
1'40"690 (151,952)
M. SCHUMACHER FERRARI
1'41"127 (151,295)

4
G. FISICHELLA BENETTON
1'41"825 (150,258)
J. TRULLI PROST
1'42"096 (149,859)

5
J. HERBERT STEWART
1'42"199 (149,708)
R. ZONTA BAR
1'42"228 (149,665)

6
P. DINIZ SAUBER
1'42"942 (148,627)
J. VILLENEUVE BAR
1'43"748 (147,473)

7
A. WURZ BENETTON
1'44"319 (146,666)
M. HAKKINEN MCLAREN
1'44"368 (146,597)

8
A. ZANARDI WILLIAMS
1'44"912 (145,837)
R. SCHUMACHER WILLIAMS
1'45"189 (145,452)

9
E. IRVINE FERRARI
1'45"218 (145,412)
D. HILL JORDAN
1'45"334 (145,252)

10
M. GENE' MINARDI
1'46"324 (143,900)
L. BADOER MINARDI
1'46"784 (143,280)

11
P. DE LA ROSA ARROWS
1'48"215 (141,385)
T. TAKAGI ARROWS
1'48"322 (141,246)

Rubens Barrichello set the second pole position of his career and Heinz-Harald Frentzen, after recovering from his crash in Canada, took Jordan to victory for the second time in its history, once again, as in 1998, in a race in the rain. For the record, Ralf Schumacher had a splendid race, starting from 16th position and ending up 4th after passing both Irvine and his elder brother 4 laps from the end. Let's have a look back at Saturday qualifying. It was raining quite hard and the dark clouds on the horizon were looking threatening.

The top teams however were not looking at the skies but at their computer monitors which were connected with the weather satellites. Barrichello and Alesi resorted to sticking their hands outside the pit garage and looking skywards to see if it was raining. The result was that these two entered the track while the others were waiting for the 'OK' from the satellites. The situation got worse during qualifying hour with the result that the drivers who went out first set the fastest times. Of the top drivers, only Coulthard (4th) and Schumacher (6th) took risks to obtain a good grid place while Hakkinen was 14th and Irvine 7th. The race saw a fantastic charge by Hakkinen who was ninth at the end of lap 1, seventh after lap 3 and second on lap 19 after diving past Schumacher and then Alesi. Immediately after, the heavens opened on lap 20 and total confusion reigned in the pits. Both Benetton drivers came in at the same time, creating panic. Irvine's mechanics fitted slick tyres by mistake and then changed them, losing almost one minute. Then everyone was out again. Hill went 'grass-cutting', Alesi went collecting sand, and so did Villeneuve (7 retirements in 7 races) and Wurz, while Gené spun into the wall. Immediately after both Hill and Zanardi came to a halt. The show continued behind the safety-car which went so fast on the wet surface that Irvine even had a spin. In the end, thanks to pit-stops by Hakkinen and Barrichello, Frentzen took the chequered flag in front of a soaking wet, but euphoric Eddie Jordan on the pit wall.

RESULTS

	DRIVER	CAR	KPH	GAP
1	H.H. Frentzen	Jordan	154.966	-
2	M. Hakkinen	McLaren	154.724	11"092
3	R. Barrichello	Stewart	154.024	43"432
4	R. Schumacher	Williams	153.980	45"475
5	M. Schumacher	Ferrari	153.928	47"881
6	E. Irvine	Ferrari	153.906	48"901
7	J. Trulli	Prost	153.715	57"771
8	O. Panis	Prost	153.699	58"531
9	R. Zonta	BAR	153.053	1"28"764
10	L. Badoer	Minardi	151.937	1 lap
11	T. Takagi	Arrows	151.179	1 lap
12	P. De La Rosa	Arrows	151.013	1 lap

RETIREMENTS

DRIVER	CAR	LAP	REASON
J. Herbert	Stewart	4	Gear
P. Diniz	Sauber	6	Gear
D. Coulthard	McLaren	9	Engine
J. Alesi	Sauber	24	Spun off
M. Gené	Minardi	25	Spun off
A. Wurz	Benetton	25	Spun off
J. Villeneuve	BAR	25	Spun off
A. Zanardi	Williams	26	Spun off
D. Hill	Jordan	31	Electrical fault
G. Fisichella	Benetton	42	Spun off

TOPSPEED

DRIVER	MAX.
Hakkinen	303.800
Frentzen	300.000
Coulthard	297.600
Hill	297.400
R. Schumacher	297.100
Irvine	296.700
Zanardi	296.300
Zonta	293.600
Wurz	292.000
Takagi	290.900
Fisichella	290.700
Herbert	290.300
Villeneuve	290.200
M. Schumacher	289.900
Barrichello	289.600
Trulli	289.000
Gené	288.200
Alesi	287.500
Panis	286.800
De La Rosa	286.700

Mika Hakkinen					40 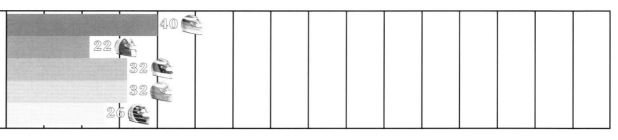							
David Coulthard		22										
Michael Schumacher			32									
Eddie Irvine			32									
Heinz H. Frentzen		26										

This GP was almost a horror film. The start had to be ... stopped after Villeneuve (gearbox) and Zanardi (stalled) were left standing on the grid. There was hardly enough time to hang out the red flags before Schumacher, who had started badly and who was down in fourth at the first curve, attacked his team-mate Irvine at Stowe, lost control of his Ferrari and went on to smash into the tyre wall. A broken right leg meant his '99 championship was over.

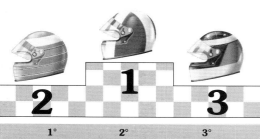

	1°	2°	3°
'90	A. Prost	T. Boutsen	A. Senna
'91	N. Mansell	G. Berger	A. Prost
'92	N. Mansell	R. Patrese	M. Brundle
'93	A. Prost	M. Schumacher	R. Patrese
'94	D. Hill	M. Schumacher	J. Alesi
'95	J. Herbert	J. Alesi	D. Coulthard
'96	J. Villeneuve	G. Berger	M. Hakkinen
'97	J. Villeneuve	J. Alesi	A. Wurz
'98	M. Schumacher	M. Hakkinen	E. Irvine

British GP

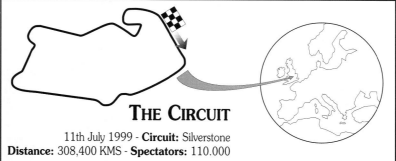

THE CIRCUIT

11th July 1999 - **Circuit:** Silverstone
Distance: 308,400 KMS - **Spectators:** 110.000

STARTING GRID

M. HAKKINEN McLAREN 1'24"804 (218,197)	1	**M. SCHUMACHER** FERRARI 1'25"223 (217,124)
D. COULTHARD McLAREN 1'25"594 (216,183)	2	**E. IRVINE** FERRARI 1'25"677 (215,974)
H.H. FRENTZEN JORDAN 1'25"991 (215,185)	3	**D. HILL** JORDAN 1'26"099 (214,915)
R. BARRICHELLO STEWART 1'26"194 (214,679)	4	**R. SCHUMACHER** WILLIAMS 1'26"438 (214,073)
J. VILLENEUVE BAR 1'26"719 (213,379)	5	**J. ALESI** SAUBER 1'26"761 (213,276)
J. HERBERT STEWART 1'26"873 (213,001)	6	**P. DINIZ** SAUBER 1'27"196 (212,212)
A. ZANARDI WILLIAMS 1'27"223 (212,146)	7	**J. TRULLI** PROST 1'27"227 (212,136)
O. PANIS PROST 1'27"543 (211,370)	8	**R. ZONTA** BAR 1'27"699 (210,994)
G. FISICHELLA BENETTON 1'27"857 (210,615)	9	**A. WURZ** BENETTON 1'28"010 (210,249)
T. TAKAGI ARROWS 1'28"037 (210,184)	10	**P. DE LA ROSA** ARROWS 1'28"148 (209,920)
L. BADOER MINARDI 1'28"695 (208,625)	11	**M. GENE'** MINARDI 1'28"772 (208,444)

Silverstone saw the return of 'horror' to F1, as well as team-mates … and maybe it was even the turning-point of the championship season as well. 'Horror' because when the number 1 Ferrari of Michael Schumacher went straight off the track on lap 1 at 250 kph, without any variation in line, and crashed into the tyre wall, the thoughts of millions of spectators immediately went back in time to the horrific incident of Senna. The impact was tremendous. Rescue crews immediately moved around the Ferrari, protecting the scene with green covers which added nail-biting anxiety to the 'horror'. Then finally we could see Schumacher lying on a stretcher waving his hand. It was the end of a nightmare. We would learn shortly after that his leg had 'only' suffered a twin fracture. Team-mates, because Hakkinen stopped while in the lead when his wheel fell off and Coulthard won from Irvine.

Third was Ralf Schumacher, who had a splendid race despite the shock of his brother's crash. Turning-point, because Schumacher will be out for at least two months. However Hakkinen and McLaren also appear to have a few problems (errors and breakages) in this championship. Maybe now it's the turn of Irvine, almost always in the points, or Coulthard, dogged by misfortune this season. Certainly the championship loses a lot with the temporary absence of the Ferrari driver but the show must go on and already thoughts were turning to a replacement for Schumacher. Badoer? Alesi? Or one of the many drivers without a drive this season? Maybe even Mika Salo, who in the past was slated to drive for Maranello? We will find out before Austria.

RESULTS

	DRIVER	CAR	KPH	GAP
1	D. Coulthard	McLaren	199.970	-
2	E. Irvine	Ferrari	199.904	1"829
3	R. Schumacher	Williams	198.987	27"411
4	H.H. Frentzen	Jordan	198.974	27"789
5	D. Hill	Jordan	198.589	38"606
6	P. Diniz	Sauber	198.056	53"643
7	G. Fisichella	Benetton	198.022	54"614
8	R. Barrichello	Stewart	197.529	1'08"590
9	J. Trulli	Prost	197.408	1'12"045
10	A. Wurz	Benetton	197.405	1'12"123
11	A. Zanardi	Williams	197.229	1'17"124
12	J. Herbert	Stewart	197.209	1'17"709
13	O. Panis	Prost	197.111	1'20"492
14	J. Alesi	Sauber	195.137	1 lap
15	M. Gené	Minardi	192.897	2 laps
16	T. Takagi	Arrows	191.751	2 laps

RETIREMENTS

DRIVER	CAR	LAP	REASON
M. Schumacher	Ferrari	0	Accident
P. De La Rosa	Arrows	0	Gear
L. Badoer	Minardi	6	Gear
J. Villeneuve	BAR	29	Axle-shaft
M. Hakkinen	McLaren	35	Retirement
R. Zonta	BAR	41	Suspension

TOPSPEED

DRIVER	MAX.
Coulthard	309.200
Frentzen	309.000
Hakkinen	308.400
Irvine	306.800
Fisichella	305.900
Zanardi	305.800
Barrichello	305.800
M. Schumacher	305.600
Hill	305.600
Herbert	305.500
Takagi	304.800
R. Schuamcher	304.700
Zonta	304.300
Wurz	303.700
Diniz	303.200
Alesi	302.600
Panis	302.300
Villeneuve	301.900
Gené	301.600
Badoer	301.500

Mika Hakkinen			44 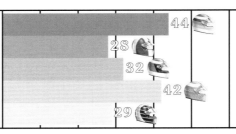					
David Coulthard		28						
Michael Schumacher		32						
Eddie Irvine			42					
Heinz H. Frentzen		29						

After replacing the injured Zonta at BAR, Mika Salo was called by Ferrari to stand in for ... the injured Schumacher. His debut for Ferrari was not exactly outstanding and the Finn finished ninth, one lap behind the winner Irvine. In the opening photo, Irvine manages to hold off a chasing David Coulthard, who had 'taken out' his team-mate Hakkinen on the first lap.

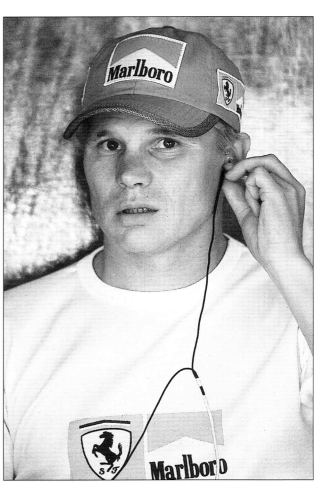

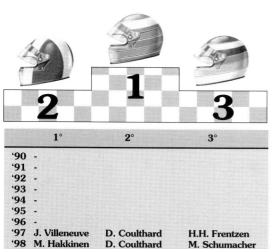

	1°	2°	3°
'90	-		
'91	-		
'92	-		
'93	-		
'94	-		
'95	-		
'96	-		
'97	J. Villeneuve	D. Coulthard	H.H. Frentzen
'98	M. Hakkinen	D. Coulthard	M. Schumacher

Austrian GP

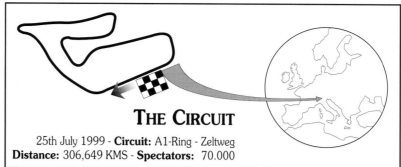

THE CIRCUIT

25th July 1999 - **Circuit:** A1-Ring - Zeltweg
Distance: 306,649 KMS - **Spectators:** 70.000

STARTING GRID

M. HAKKINEN McLaren 1'10"954 (219,134)	(1)	**D. COULTHARD** McLaren 1'11"153 (218,521)
E. IRVINE FERRARI 1'11"973 (216,031)	(2)	**H.H. FRENTZEN** JORDAN 1'12"266 (215,155)
R. BARRICHELLO STEWART 1'12"342 (214,929)	(3)	**J. HERBERT** STEWART 1'12"488 (214,496)
M. SALO FERRARI 1'12"514 (214,419)	(4)	**R. SCHUMACHER** WILLIAMS 1'12"515 (214,416)
J. VILLENEUVE BAR 1'12"833 (213,480)	(5)	**A. WURZ** BENETTON 1'12"850 (213,430)
D. HILL JORDAN 1'12"901 (213,281)	(6)	**G. FISICHELLA** BENETTON 1'12"924 (213,214)
J. TRULLI PROST 1'12"999 (212,995)	(7)	**A. ZANARDI** WILLIAMS 1'13"101 (212,698)
R. ZONTA BAR 1'13"172 (212,491)	(8)	**P. DINIZ** SAUBER 1'13"223 (212,343)
J. ALESI SAUBER 1'13"226 (212,334)	(9)	**O. PANIS** PROST 1'13"457 (211,667)
L. BADOER MINARDI 1'13"606 (211,238)	(10)	**T. TAKAGI** ARROWS 1'13"641 (211,138)
P. DE LA ROSA ARROWS 1'14"139 (209,720)	(11)	**M. GENE'** MINARDI 1'14"363 (209,088)

Qualifying went as usual. Front row for McLaren-Mercedes and 3rd place for Irvine's Ferrari, while Mika Salo, with the number 3 car, qualified in 7th place. Away they go and Coulthard, not new to such exploits, touches the McLaren of team-mate Hakkinen at the second curve in a rather hazardous attempt at passing him on the inside.

Coulthard continues followed by Barrichello and Irvine while Hakkinen has to stop in the pits and rejoins the race in last position. The incident between the two McLarens created a 'bottleneck' behind and it was Salo who paid the penalty, running into Herbert and damaging his nose-cone. The newly-wed Finn had to pit and he also rejoined the race at the back. Hakkinen returns to the track in a fury and starts scything his way through the field to a 3rd place at the flag, despite a slightly badly-handling McLaren. The Finn was the real hero of the day, as he was a few weeks before in France with another spectacular recovery and fourteen overtaking manoeuvres that had taken him to the runner-up slot. Back to the racing. Coulthard was still in the lead, with Barrichello and Irvine following 15 seconds behind, but between laps 38 and 40 everything changed. After his pit-stop, Barrichello lost a number of positions and then came to a halt with engine failure 15 laps from the end. Coulthard stopped for his pit-stop while at Ferrari, Ross Brawn ordered Eddie Irvine to stay out so that the Ulsterman would gain as much time as possible in the few laps with a light fuel load.

This was the winning strategy. When Irvine pitted, thanks to a very rapid stop, he managed to get back on the track ahead of Coulthard and to keep him under control until the chequered flag. The Irishman sprinted to his second Formula 1 victory. There isn't much to say about the rest. Once again (9 times out of 9) Villeneuve failed to finish a race, while Alesi and Zanardi incredibly rolled to a halt out on the circuit with no fuel because they had failed to hear the pit radio. Salo was ninth while Frentzen was again in the points with fourth place.

RESULTS

	DRIVER	CAR	KPH	GAP
1	E. Irvine	Ferrari	208.587	-
2	D. Coulthard	McLaren	208.575	0"313
3	M. Hakkinen	McLaren	207.712	22"282
4	H.H. Frentzen	Jordan	206.526	52"803
5	A. Wurz	Benetton	206.004	1'06"358
6	P. Diniz	Sauber	205.828	1'10"933
7	J. Trulli	Prost	205.026	1 lap
8	D. Hill	Jordan	204.981	1 lap
9	M. Salo	Ferrari	204.747	1 lap
10	O. Panis	Prost	204.582	1 lap
11	M. Gené	Minardi	202.863	1 lap
12	G. Fisichella	Benetton	205.240	3 laps
13	L. Badoer	Minardi	198.061	3 laps
14	J. Herbert	Stewart	194.333	4 laps
15	R. Zonta	BAR	204.094	8 laps

RETIREMENTS

DRIVER	CAR	LAP	REASON
R. Schumacher	Williams	8	Spun off
T. Takagi	Arrows	25	Engine
J. Villeneuve	BAR	34	Axle-shaft
A. Zanardi	Williams	35	Fuel
P. De La Rosa	Arrows	38	Spun off
J. Alesi	Sauber	49	Fuel
R. Barrichello	Stewart	55	Engine

TOPSPEED

DRIVER	MAX.
Wurz	307.000
Fisichella	305.600
Alesi	303.600
Hill	303.300
Hakkinen	302.000
Coulthard	301.000
Herbert	300.900
Diniz	299.500
Salo	298.900
Irvine	298.000
Barrichello	298.000
Frentzen	297.100
Zanardi	297.000
Zonta	296.700
De La Rosa	295.500
Panis	295.200
Trulli	295.000
Takagi	295.000
Gené	292.600
Badoer	291.800

Mika Hakkinen				44 							
David Coulthard			30								
Michael Schumacher			32								
Eddie Irvine					52						
Heinz H. Frentzen			33								

Damon Hill was the protagonist of the German GP. After announcing his retirement half-way through the season and then going back on his decision, at Hockenheim Hill inexplicably retired on lap 13, angering his boss Eddie Jordan and further disappointing all his fans. A fantastic podium and 1-2 victory for Ferrari with Irvine the winner, followed home by Salo. It was the first podium of the Finn's career and the first time he had ever been in the lead of a GP.

196

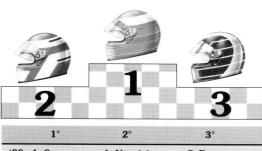

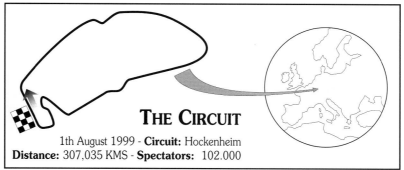

German GP

THE CIRCUIT

1th August 1999 - **Circuit:** Hockenheim
Distance: 307,035 KMS - **Spectators:** 102.000

	1°	2°	3°
'90	A. Senna	A. Nannini	G. Berger
'91	N. Mansell	R. Patrese	J. Alesi
'92	N. Mansell	A. Senna	M. Schumacher
'93	A. Prost	M. Schumacher	M. Brundell
'94	G. Berger	O. Panis	E. Bernard
'95	M. Schumacher	D. Coulthard	G. Berger
'96	D. Hill	J. Alesi	J. Villeneuve
'97	G. Berger	M. Schumacher	M. Hakkinen
'98	M. Hakkinen	D. Coulthard	J. Villenuve

STARTING GRID

1
M. HAKKINEN McLAREN
1'42"950 (238,590)

H.H. FRENTZEN JORDAN
1'43"000 (238,474)

2
D. COULTHARD McLAREN
1'43"288 (237,809)

M. SALO FERRARI
1'43"577 (237,145)

3
E. IRVINE FERRARI
1'43"769 (236,707)

R. BARRICHELLO STEWART
1'43"938 (236,322)

4
O. PANIS PROST
1'43"979 (236,228)

D. HILL JORDAN
1'44"001 (236,178)

5
J. TRULLI PROST
1'44"209 (235,707)

G. FISICHELLA BENETTON
1'44"338 (235,416)

6
R. SCHUMACHER WILLIAMS
1'44"468 (235,123)

J. VILLENEUVE BAR
1'44"508 (235,033)

7
A. WURZ BENETTON
1'44"522 (235,001)

A. ZANARDI WILLIAMS
1'45"034 (233,856)

8
M. GENE' MINARDI
1'45"331 (233,196)

P. DINIZ SAUBER
1'45"335 (233,187)

9
J. HERBERT STEWART
1'45"454 (232,924)

R. ZONTA BAR
1'45"460 (232,911)

10
L. BADOER MINARDI
1'45"917 (231,906)

P. DE LA ROSA ARROWS
1'45"935 (231,867)

11
J. ALESI SAUBER
1'45"962 (231,808)

T. TAKAGI ARROWS
1'46"209 (231,269)

The local air failed to have any beneficial effects on Team McLaren-Mercedes, which as usual was superb in qualifying, but then dogged by misfortune and errors during the race. First, Hakkinen's pit-stop lasted more than 23 seconds because of a problem with the fuel valve; then he went out again and on that same lap, he had a rear-tyre failure, pirouetting four times before slamming into the barriers in the legendary Motodrom. Not to be outdone, Coulthard again showed his limitations: on lap 5 he damaged his wing after tapping Salo, then got a stop-and-go penalty for cutting part of a chicane while trying to overtake Panis. All this meant that Eddie Irvine cruised to his second win on the run (his third in '99 and in his career), with a fantastic Mika Salo second on the podium and Frentzen third.

The driver of the day however was Salo. Despite it being only the second time he had driven a Ferrari, he was a major player right from the start, battling aggressively but cleanly with Coulthard and then obeying team orders to let Irvine through on lap 25, when he was leading a race for the first time in his career. The German GP concluded with a memorable Ferrari 1-2 (the 45th in its history), and Irvine now had an eight point lead in the championship over Hakkinen, with Ferrari 24 points ahead of McLaren in the Constructors' championship. The race saw another excellent performance from Frentzen, second fastest in qualifying, third at the end of the race and third in the championship standings. For the rest, mention should go to Villeneuve (10 races and 10 retirements) and to Hill, who made a bizarre decision on lap 14 not to continue as he was unhappy with his brakes.

RESULTS

	DRIVER	CAR	KPH	GAP
1	E. Irvine	Ferrari	224.723	-
2	M. Salo	Ferrari	224.677	1"007
3	H.H. Frentzen	Jordan	224.486	5"195
4	R. Schumacher	Williams	224.140	12"809
5	D. Coulthard	McLaren	223.957	16"823
6	O. Panis	Prost	223.367	29"879
7	A. Wurz	Benetton	223.211	33"333
8	J. Alesi	Sauber	221.513	1'11"291
9	M. Gené	Minardi	219.881	1'48"318
10	L. Badoer	Minardi	219.036	1 lap
11	J. Herbert	Stewart	223.091	5 laps

RETIREMENTS

DRIVER	CAR	LAP	REASON
P. Diniz	Sauber	0	Crashed
J. Villeneuve	BAR	0	Crashed
R. Barrichello	Stewart	6	Gear
G. Fisichella	Benetton	7	Suspension
J. Trulli	Prost	10	Engine
D. Hill	Jordan	13	Retirement
T. Takagi	Arrows	15	Engine
R. Zonta	BAR	20	Engine
A. Zanardi	Williams	21	Clutch
M. Hakkinen	McLaren	25	Crashed
P. De La Rosa	Arrows	37	Crashed

TOPSPEED

DRIVER	MAX.
Coulthard	357.400
Barrichello	355.200
Alesi	355.200
Herbert	354.700
Panis	352.900
Hill	352.300
Irvine	351.700
Hakkinen	351.100
Frentzen	350.600
Trulli	350.000
Salo	349.500
Wurz	348.400
Gené	347.400
Zonta	346.300
Badoer	345.100
De La Rosa	343.100
Fisichella	342.600
R. Schumacher	342.400
Zanardi	338.600
Takagi	337.600

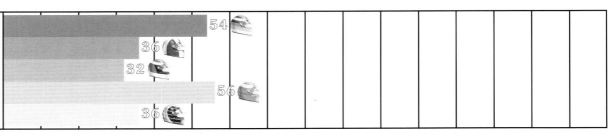

Mika Hakkinen				54						
David Coulthard		36								
Michael Schumacher		32								
Eddie Irvine				56						
Heinz H. Frentzen		36								

Hakkinen returned to the top of the podium in Hungary, while Frentzen again scored precious points with the Jordan in fourth. Outside the circuit, a subtle battle of faxes and press releases was taking place between the managers of the two Ferrari drivers, Enrico Zanarini (with Irvine in the photo on the left) and Willi Weber (right with Schumacher), who both stressed how good their drivers were.

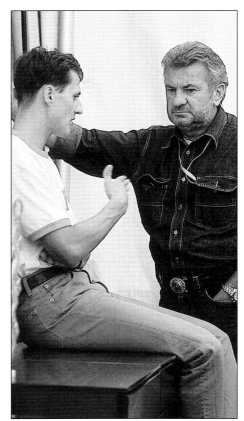

198

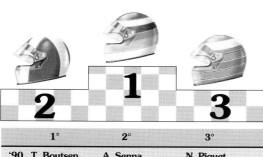

Hungarian GP

	1°	2°	3°
'90	T. Boutsen	A. Senna	N. Piquet
'91	A. Senna	N. Mansell	R. Patrese
'92	A. Senna	N. Mansell	G. Berger
'93	D. Hill	R. Patrese	G. Berger
'94	M. Schumacher	D. Hill	J. Verstappen
'95	D. Hill	D. Coulthard	G. Berger
'96	J. Villeneuve	D. Hill	J. Alesi
'97	J. Villeneuve	D. Hill	J. Herbert
'98	M. Schumacher	D. Coulthard	J. Villeneuve

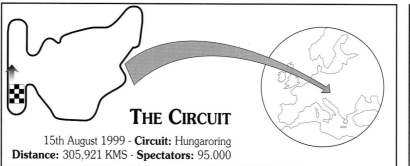

THE CIRCUIT

15th August 1999 - **Circuit:** Hungaroring
Distance: 305,921 KMS - **Spectators:** 95.000

STARTING GRID

1
M. HAKKINEN McLAREN
1'18"156 (183,003)

E. IRVINE FERRARI
1'18"263 (182,753)

2
D. COULTHARD McLAREN
1'18"384 (182,470)

G. FISICHELLA BENETTON
1'18"515 (182,166)

3
H.H. FRENTZEN JORDAN
1'18"664 (181,821)

D. HILL JORDAN
1'18"667 (181,814)

4
A. WURZ BENETTON
1'18"733 (181,662)

R. BARRICHELLO STEWART
1'19"095 (180,830)

5
J. VILLENEUVE BAR
1'19"127 (180,757)

J. HERBERT STEWART
1'19"389 (180,160)

6
J. ALESI SAUBER
1'19"390 (180,158)

P. DINIZ SAUBER
1'19"782 (179,273)

7
J. TRULLI PROST
1'19"788 (179,260)

O. PANIS PROST
1'19"841 (179,041)

8
A. ZANARDI WILLIAMS
1'19"924 (178,955)

R. SCHUMACHER WILLIAMS
1'19"945 (178,907)

9
R. ZONTA BAR
1'20"060 (178,651)

M. SALO FERRARI
1'20"369 (177,964)

10
L. BADOER MINARDI
1'20"961 (176,662)

P. DE LA ROSA ARROWS
1'21"328 (175,865)

11
T. TAKAGI ARROWS
1'21"675 (175,118)

M. GENE' MINARDI
1'21"867 (174,707)

The week before the Hungarian Grand Prix was marked by a long-distance 'duel' between the managers of Schumacher and Irvine with Ferrari in the middle trying to play things down.
"Irvine's two successive victories are also due to Schumacher's development work on the car",
"Irvine won because the McLaren-Mercedes drivers made mistakes" declared Willi Weber, Michael Schumacher's manager.
"Irvine is a driver who deserves to be number 1 in a team",
"The time has come for Irvine to stop being number 2 driver" replied Enrico Zanarini, Irvine's manager.
And so it was, that between press releases and declarations by journalists, the F1 Circus arrived in Budapest, where the track soon focused the minds of the leading contenders onto the job in hand.
In qualifying, Hakkinen stormed to pole position, but Irvine was just 107/1000ths of a second behind him. Coulthard was next up with the Benetton of Fisichella alongside. The third row was made up of the two Jordans, which were running on new, ultra-soft tyres. Mika Salo was a disaster, way down in 18th position.

At the lights, Hakkinen powered away followed by Irvine.
The Finn remained in control of the entire 78 lap race.
He was followed by Irvine until lap 62, when the Ulsterman, under pressure from Coulthard, missed his braking point and went on the grass, losing a vital second place.
The only real excitement in this race was Irvine's and Coulthard's fantastic simultaneous pit-stop, when the two rivals came in and went out in exactly the same positions after a stop of just 7.3 seconds.
The 'prize' for the unluckiest driver again went to Jacques Villeneuve, who failed to finish a GP for the 11th time in 11 races.
Not to be outdone was Jean Alesi who, after starting from row 6 with 11th fastest time, worked his way up to 4th place ... but then rolled to a halt with an empty fuel tank.
Back in the pits, Alesi worked himself up into a frenzy, took his anger out on anyone within earshot and told the press that he would be leaving Sauber at the end of the year.
One team that continued to notch up the points was Jordan, now firmly in third place in the championship.
With two-thirds of the championship over, both BAR and Minardi were still without a point.

RESULTS

	DRIVER	CAR	KPH	GAP
1	M. Hakkinen	McLaren	172.524	-
2	D. Coulthard	McLaren	172.262	9"706
3	E. Irvine	Ferrari	171.791	27"228
4	H.H. Frentzen	Jordan	171.668	31"815
5	R. Barrichello	Stewart	171.348	43"808
6	D. Hill	Jordan	171.031	55"726
7	A. Wurz	Benetton	170.891	1'01"012
8	J. Trulli	Prost	169.733	1 lap
9	R. Schumacher	Williams	169.493	1 lap
10	O. Panis	Prost	169.142	1 lap
11	J. Herbert	Stewart	168.535	1 lap
12	M. Salo	Ferrari	167.906	2 laps
13	R. Zonta	BAR	167.878	2 laps
14	L. Badoer	Minardi	167.347	2 laps
15	P. De La Rosa	Arrows	167.138	2 laps
16	J. Alesi	Sauber	170.121	3 laps
17	M. Gené	Minardi	164.963	3 laps

RETIREMENTS

DRIVER	CAR	LAP	REASON
A. Zanardi	Williams	10	Differential
P. Diniz	Sauber	19	Spun off
T. Takagi	Arrows	26	Axle-shaft
G. Fisichella	Benetton	52	Fuel pressure
J. Villeneuve	BAR	60	Clutch

TOPSPEED

DRIVER	MAX.
Coulthard	292.700
R. Schumacher	289.900
Villeneuve	289.500
Wurz	288.000
Hakkinen	287.900
Fisichella	287.600
Barrichello	287.300
Irvine	286.500
Hill	286.400
Salo	286.300
Frentzen	286.200
Alesi	286.100
Zonta	286.100
Zanardi	285.900
Diniz	285.400
Herbert	284.500
Trulli	283.000
De La Rosa	281.900
Badoer	281.700
Gené	281.700

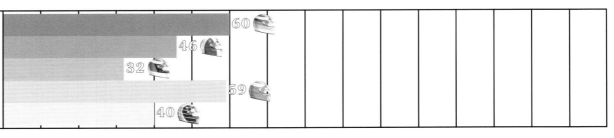

Mika Hakkinen			60							
David Coulthard		46								
Michael Schumacher	32									
Eddie Irvine			59							
Heinz H. Frentzen	40									

Like in Austria, in Belgium the two McLarens risked being eliminated at the first curve. Things went better at Spa however because they came first and second with Coulthard ahead of championship leader Hakkinen … and this was a small gift for Ferrari. Villeneuve finally saw the chequered flag in Belgium and so did the two Williams drivers, Ralf Schumacher and Alex Zanardi.

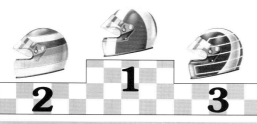

	1°	2°	3°
'90	A. Senna	A. Prost	G. Berger
'91	A. Senna	G. Berger	N. Piquet
'92	M. Schumacher	N. Mansell	R. Patrese
'93	D. Hill	M. Schumacher	A. Prost
'94	D. Hill	M. Hakkinen	J. Verstappen
'95	M. Schumacher	D. Hill	M. Brundle
'96	M. Schumacher	J. Villeneuve	M. Hakkinen
'97	M. Schumacher	G. Fisichella	M. hakkinen
'98	D. Hill	R. Schumacher	J. Alesi

Belgian GP

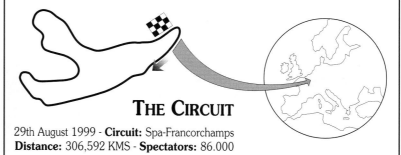

THE CIRCUIT

29th August 1999 - **Circuit:** Spa-Francorchamps
Distance: 306,592 KMS - **Spectators:** 86.000

STARTING GRID

1
M. HAKKINEN McLAREN
1'50"329 (227,364)
D. COULTHARD McLAREN
1'50"484 (227,045)

2
H.H. FRENTZEN JORDAN
1'51"332 (225,315)
D. HILL JORDAN
1'51"372 (225,234)

3
R. SCHUMACHER WILLIAMS
1'51"414 (225,149)
E. IRVINE FERRARI
1'51"895 (224,182)

4
R. BARRICHELLO STEWART
1'51"974 (224,023)
A. ZANARDI WILLIAMS
1'52"014 (223,943)

5
M. SALO FERRARI
1'52"124 (223,724)
J. HERBERT STEWART
1'52"164 (223,644)

6
J. VILLENEUVE BAR
1'52"235 (223,502)
J. TRULLI PROST
1'52"644 (222,691)

7
G. FISICHELLA BENETTON
1'52"762 (222,458)
R. ZONTA BAR
1'52"840 (222,304)

8
A. WURZ BENETTON
1'52"847 (222,290)
J. ALESI SAUBER
1'52"921 (222,145)

9
O. PANIS PROST
1'53"148 (221,699)
P. DINIZ SAUBER
1'53"778 (220,471)

10
T. TAKAGI ARROWS
1'54"099 (219,851)
L. BADOER MINARDI
1'54"197 (219,663)

11
M. GENE' MINARDI
1'54"557 (218,972)
P. DE LA ROSA ARROWS
1'54"579 (218,930)

Thank you David! Had it not been for Coulthard, the championship would have probably been over by now. What would the points table have looked like if David had not made contact with Mika in Austria and let him through in Belgium? Instead, with Schumacher out with a broken leg, and thanks to the 'non-strategy' of Hakkinen and Coulthard, six drivers could in theory still win the championship with just four rounds left.

Let's get back to the Spa weekend, which for a change was sunny. In qualifying the McLarens dominated with alarming technical superiority, and they were followed by the Jordans which were both faster and had a better set-up than the Ferraris which lined up in 6th and ninth place. Finally both Williams managed to perform well and Schumacher and Zanardi were on rows 3 and 4.

At the start, Hakkinen looked as if he was going to jump the lights, but he slowed, letting Coulthard through into the first right-hander after the pits. On the pit-wall the McLaren team closed its collective eyes and waited

for a replay of Austria. Instead, David managed to hold onto that all-important first position which he would maintain until the flag, without there being much contact between the two. Hakkinen realised it was not going to be the right day to take risks and slotted in behind in second place, which he too would hold until the flag. All was not well inside the Finn however, as he did everything to ignore his team-mate on the podium. Irvine was never even in a position to take on Hakkinen, and even had to thank Salo for holding up the recovery of Ralf Schumacher in the Williams. As usual, Frentzen was superb, picking up another third place. The German was now fourth in the table, 20 points behind leader Hakkinen. Jacques Villeneuve finally succeeded in finishing a GP for the first time this year. After the race, the Canadian jokingly commented with journalists on his magnificent exploit. It is worth mentioning however that Jacques and his team-mate Zonta had been involved in two frightening crashes during qualifying when they went off the track at more than 250 kph, destroying both BAR cars.

RESULTS

	DRIVER	CAR	KPH	GAP
1	D. Coulthard	McLaren	214.595	-
2	M. Hakkinen	McLaren	214.159	10"469
3	H.H. Frentzen	Jordan	213.209	33"433
4	E. Irvine	Ferrari	212.736	44"948
5	R. Schumacher	Williams	212.606	48"067
6	D. Hill	Jordan	212.328	54"916
7	M. Salo	Ferrari	212.273	56"249
8	A. Zanardi	Williams	211.835	1'07"022
9	J. Alesi	Sauber	211.557	1'13"848
10	R. Barrichello	Stewart	211.278	1'20"742
11	G. Fisichella	Benetton	210.816	1'32"195
12	J. Trulli	Prost	210.657	1'36"154
13	O. Panis	Prost	210.440	1'41"543
14	A. Wurz	Benetton	209.792	1'57"745
15	J. Villeneuve	BAR	209.447	1 lap
16	M. Gené	Minardi	208.240	1 lap

RETIREMENTS

DRIVER	CAR	LAP	REASON
T. Takagi	Arrows	0	Engine
P. Diniz	Sauber	19	Suspension
J. Herbert	Stewart	27	Brakes
R. Zonta	BAR	33	Gear
L. Badoer	Minardi	33	Crashed
P. De La Rosa	Arrows	35	Transmission

TOPSPEED

DRIVER	MAX.
Coulthard	331.600
Frentzen	330.900
Hakkinen	330.100
Wurz	329.700
R. Schumacher	327.800
Fisichella	327.000
Panis	326.300
Irvine	325.900
Barrichello	325.900
Trulli	325.700
Zanardi	325.600
Alesi	325.500
Hill	325.500
Diniz	325.100
De La Rosa	324.100
Salo	323.900
Herbert	322.900
Takagi	322.800
Badoer	322.400
Villeneuve	321.200

Mika Hakkinen							60								
David Coulthard						48									
Michael Schumacher				32											
Eddie Irvine							60								
Heinz H. Frentzen					50										

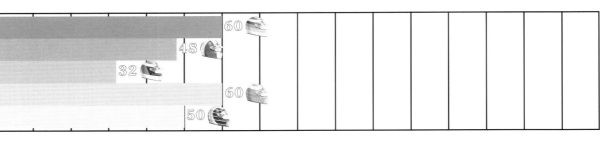

Frentzen celebrates his second win of the season and Salo shows his joy in front of more than 100,000 Monza tifosi. The Brazilian footballer Ronaldo paid a visit to his fellow-countryman Barrichello. Hakkinen's GP came to an end when his McLaren spun off coming out of the first chicane.

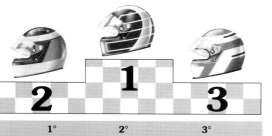

	1°	2°	3°
'90	A. Senna	A. Prost	G. Berger
'91	N. Mansell	A. Senna	A. Prost
'92	A. Senna	M. Brundle	M. Schumacher
'93	D. Hill	J. Alesi	M. Andretti
'94	D. Hill	G. Berger	M. Hakkinen
'95	J. Herbert	M. Hakkinen	H.H. Frentzen
'96	M. Schumacher	J. Alesi	M.Hakkinen
'97	D. Coulthard	J. Alesi	H.H. Frentzen
'98	M. Schumacher	E. Irvine	R. Schumacher

Italian GP

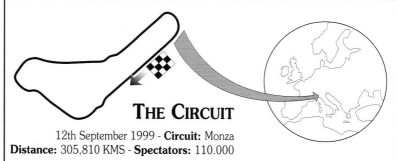

THE CIRCUIT

12th September 1999 - **Circuit:** Monza
Distance: 305,810 KMS - **Spectators:** 110.000

STARTING GRID

M. HAKKINEN McLAREN
1'22"432 (251,990)

(1) **H.H. FRENTZEN** JORDAN
1'22"926 (250,488)

D. COULTHARD McLAREN
1'23"177 (249,732)

(2) **A. ZANARDI** WILLIAMS
1'23"432 (248,969)

R. SCHUMACHER WILLIAMS
1'23"636 (248,362)

(3) **M. SALO** FERRARI
1'23"657 (248,300)

R. BARRICHELLO STEWART
1'23"739 (248,056)

(4) **E. IRVINE** FERRARI
1'23"765 (247,979)

D. HILL JORDAN
1'23"979 (247,348)

(5) **O. PANIS** PROST
1'24"016 (247,239)

J. VILLENEUVE BAR
1'24"188 (246,734)

(6) **J. TRULLI** PROST
1'24"293 (246,426)

J. ALESI SAUBER
1'24"591 (245,558)

(7) **A. WURZ** BENETTON
1'24"593 (245,552)

J. HERBERT STEWART
1'24"594 (245,549)

(8) **P. DINIZ** SAUBER
1'24"596 (245,544)

G. FISICHELLA BENETTON
1'24"862 (244,774)

(9) **R. ZONTA** BAR
1'25"114 (244,049)

L. BADOER MINARDI
1'25"348 (243,380)

(10) **M. GENE'** MINARDI
1'25"695 (242,395)

P. DE LA ROSA ARROWS
1'26"383 (240,464)

(11) **T. TAKAGI** ARROWS
1'26"509 (240,114)

It's 2.45 pm and the Italian GP is approaching its half-way point, without having offered much in the way of entertainment. Hundreds of journalists are probably finishing the first draft of their articles and we can imagine the contents: "boring race ... no surprises ... the result was the same as the starting-grid. No problems for the winner Hakkinen ... followed by Frentzen, Ralf Schumacher in the Williams and then Salo in the Ferrari, ahead of Irvine, just like in qualifying". The only excitement comes from Takagi with the Arrows, who was clearly bored with the race as well and was enjoying himself by punting his rivals off at the chicanes. Lap after lap, the gap between the leaders remained unchanged: with today's F1 cars, it is difficult to catch up or pull out a lead on one's rivals at Monza, unless ... something unexpected happens. Something unexpected did happen on lap 30. Hakkinen, leading Frentzen by more than 7 seconds, arrived at the first chicane at the end of the start-finish straight,

and to the amazement of the more than 100,000 spectators, lost control and ended up in the gravel. With a gesture of anger, he threw away his steering-wheel and gloves and made his way back to the pits. (Driver error? Mechanical problems? Or both together?) Then, under the watchful eye of the TV camera, he knelt down with his head in his hands and desperately burst into tears. Never mind, Mika! With that gesture, you demonstrated that modern-day F1 is not only made up of computers, telemetry and robots. Back on the track, nothing changed until the end. Congratulations go to Frentzen for his second win of 1999, as well as to Schumacher Jr. and Salo, who has become a favourite of the Ferrari fans in just a short time. And Irvine? Rather an opaque performance, to say the least, with everyone wondering how it is possible that a week before, he was faster than everyone else in Monza private testing. What about Takagi? After several attempts, he finally managed to punt off Badoer in the Minardi on lap 24 and then spun off himself on lap 36 at the same chicane.

RESULTS

	DRIVER	CAR	KPH	GAP
1	H.H. Frentzen	Jordan	237.938	-
2	R. Schumacher	Williams	237.770	3"272
3	M. Salo	Ferrari	237.326	11"932
4	R. Barrichello	Stewart	237.034	17"630
5	D. Coulthard	McLaren	237.008	18"142
6	E. Irvine	Ferrari	236.536	27"402
7	A. Zanardi	Williams	236.503	28"047
8	J. Villeneuve	BAR	236.806	41"797
9	J. Alesi	Sauber	235.766	42"198
10	D. Hill	Jordan	235.078	56"259
11	O. Panis	Prost	235.090	1 lap

RETIREMENTS

DRIVER	CAR	LAP	REASON
M. Gené	Minardi	0	Accident
G. Fisichella	Benetton	1	Crashed
P. Diniz	Sauber	1	Spun off
A. Wurz	Benetton	11	Electrical fault
L. Badoer	Minardi	23	Accident
R. Zonta	BAR	25	Brakes
J. Trulli	Prost	29	Gear
M. Hakkinen	McLaren	29	Crashed
T. Takagi	Arrows	35	Crashed
P. De La Rosa	Arrows	35	Suspension
J. Herbert	Stewart	40	Clutch

TOPSPEED

DRIVER	MAX.
Coulthard	361.800
Herbert	355.000
Trulli	354.300
Alesi	351.600
Barrichello	351.500
Hakkinen	351.100
Wurz	350.100
Hill	349.400
Fisichella	349.000
Panis	348.600
Villeneuve	348.400
Salo	347.600
Zonta	347.200
Frentzen	345.900
Irvine	345.600
Badoer	345.300
De La Rosa	342.400
Takagi	341.900
R.Schumacher	338.800
Diniz	337.700

Mika Hakkinen						62							
David Coulthard				48									
Michael Schumacher		32											
Eddie Irvine						60							
Heinz H. Frentzen					50								

How on earth Diniz didn't suffer any injuries from such a serious incident must have wondered millions of TV viewers when they saw the Brazilian driver giving the thumbs up to show he was OK after being extricated from the wreckage of his Sauber. It all seemed plain sailing for Frentzen, who led from lap 1 to 32, when an electronic problem brought his race to an end. Two of the three podium places were taken by Stewart drivers.

	1°	2°	3°
'90	-	-	-
'91	-	-	-
'92	-	-	-
'93	A. Senna	D. Hill	A. Prost
'94	M. Schumacher	D. Hill	M. Hakkinen
'95	M. Schumacher	J. Alesi	D. Coulthard
'96	J. Villeneuve	M. Schumacher	D. Coulthard
'97	M. Hakkinen	D. Coulthard	J. Villeneuve
'98	-	-	-

European GP

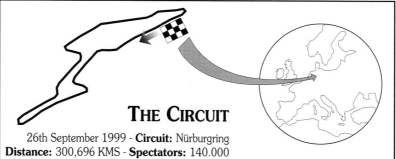

The Circuit

26th September 1999 - **Circuit:** Nürburgring
Distance: 300,696 KMS - **Spectators:** 140.000

Starting Grid

H.H. Frentzen Jordan 1'19"910 (205,251)	**D. Coulthard** McLaren 1'20"176 (204,570)
M. Hakkinen McLaren 1'20"376 (204,061)	**R. Schumacher** Williams 1'20"444 (203,888)
O. Panis Prost 1'20"638 (203,398)	**G. Fisichella** Benetton 1'20"781 (203,038)
D. Hill Jordan 1'20"818 (202,945)	**J. Villeneuve** BAR 1'20"825 (202,927)
E. Irvine Ferrari 1'20"842 (202,885)	**J. Trulli** Prost 1'20"965 (202,576)
A. Wurz Benetton 1'21"144 (202,130)	**M. Salo** Ferrari 1'21"314 (201,707)
P. Diniz Sauber 1'21"345 (201,630)	**J. Herbert** Stewart 1'21"379 (201,546)
R. Barrichello Stewart 1'21"490 (201,271)	**J. Alesi** Sauber 1'21"634 (200,916)
R. Zonta BAR 1'22"267 (199,370)	**A. Zanardi** Williams 1'22"284 (199,329)
L. Badoer Minardi 1'22"631 (198,492)	**M. Gene'** Minardi 1'22"760 (198,183)
T. Takagi Arrows 1'23"401 (196,660)	**P. De La Rosa** Arrows 1'23"698 (195,962)

"What a mess!" might well have been the first words of Eddie Irvine a few years back when he arrived in Ferrari. This also just about summed up everything about the European GP held at the Nurburgring in September. Hill slowed suddenly at the first corner of lap 1, creating havoc behind in the pack. Wurz managed to avoid him, went into Diniz's Sauber, which flipped, landing upside down on the grass. The situation was dramatic because the Sauber's roll hoop was broken and Diniz was underneath the car. Luckily he was extricated by the crash crew without a scratch. The race restarted with Frentzen in the lead, a position he would hold easily until lap 30 when he stopped with electronic problems. On lap 17, it began to rain, but only on part of the circuit and at the pits, while things started to get hectic out on the track. Some drivers came in to fit rain tyres while others decided to stay out on slicks, slithering around like rally cars on the wet part of the circuit. Irvine also decided to come in but in all the confusion he found that his team had only made three tyres available for the pit-stop.

The comedy show was seen live all around the world. It was raining and then it stopped. It started to rain again and the pit-stops continued with alarming frequency, with the result that Hakkinen was 10th and Irvine 7th. The drivers to benefit from all this confusion were those who did not panic in the pits, such as Ralf Schumacher who took the lead on lap 38. The German stopped for tyres on lap 44, losing the lead to Fisichella but he spun off on lap 50 and it was Herbert who led the race until the chequered flag. So victory went to Johnny Herbert with the Stewart, followed by Trulli in the Prost and Barrichello with the second Stewart. It was a triumph for Jackie Stewart who scored the final win of his career at the Nurburgring way back in'73. It's also worth mentioning that Minardi scored a vital one point or sixth place with Gené. They almost scored three for fourth place with Badoer, who unfortunately stopped with a broken gearbox ten laps from the end. And Hakkinen? An undistinguished fifth place that moved him into a two-point lead over Irvine in the world championship.

Results

	DRIVER	CAR	KPH	GAP
1	J. Herbert	Stewart	177.044	-
2	J. Trulli	Prost	176.392	22"619
3	R. Barrichello	Stewart	176.385	22"866
4	R. Schumacher	Williams	175.908	39"508
5	M. Hakkinen	McLaren	175.240	1'02"950
6	M. Gené	Minardi	175.178	1'05"154
7	E. Irvine	Ferrari	175.134	1'06"683
8	R. Zonta	BAR	173.947	1 lap
9	O. Panis	Prost	173.686	1 lap
10	J. Villeneuve	BAR	173.839	5 laps

Retirements

DRIVER	CAR	LAP	REASON
A. Wurz	Benetton	0	Accident
D. Hill	Jordan	0	Accident
P. Diniz	Sauber	0	Accident
A. Zanardi	Williams	10	Spun off
H.H. Frentzen	Jordan	32	Electrical fault
J. Alesi	Sauber	35	Gear
D. Coulthard	McLaren	37	Crashed
T. Takagi	Arrows	42	Crashed
M. Salo	Ferrari	44	Brakes
G. Fisichella	Benetton	48	Crashed
P. De La Rosa	Arrows	52	Gear
L. Badoer	Minardi	53	Gear

Topspeed

DRIVER	MAX.
Hakkinen	312.500
Irvine	305.700
Barrichello	305.500
Salo	303.900
Coulthard	303.700
R.Schumacher	303.000
Zanardi	302.600
Panis	302.100
Fisichella	301.600
Herbert	301.300
Zonta	301.100
Trulli	300.500
Alesi	299.800
Villeneuve	299.800
Frentzen	299.700
Badoer	298.200
Gené	297.000
De La Rosa	296.600
Takagi	293.100

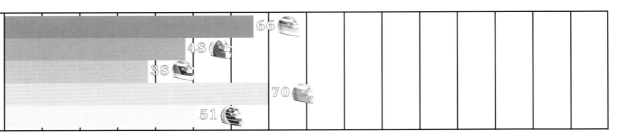

Mika Hakkinen												
David Coulthard												
Michael Schumacher												
Eddie Irvine												
Heinz H. Frentzen												

Mika Hakkinen 66
David Coulthard 48
Michael Schumacher 38
Eddie Irvine 70
Heinz H. Frentzen 51

The start of the Malaysian GP, with the futuristic structure of the new Sepang circuit in the background. The victorious arrival of Eddie Irvine, with the Ferrari mechanics celebrating on the pit-wall. Their joy was short-lived after the two Ferraris were disqualified for alleged 'barge-board' irregularities (see photo).

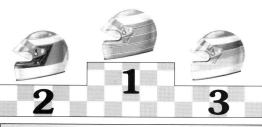

Malaysia GP

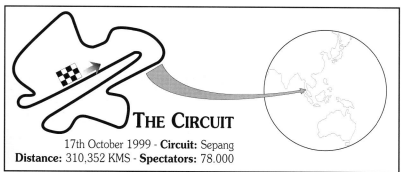

THE CIRCUIT

17th October 1999 - **Circuit:** Sepang
Distance: 310,352 KMS - **Spectators:** 78.000

STARTING GRID

M. SCHUMACHER FERRARI
1'39"688 (200,136)
(1)

E. IRVINE FERRARI
1'40"635 (198,253)

D. COULTHARD MCLAREN
1'40"806 (197,917)
(2)

M. HAKKINEN MCLAREN
1'40"866 (197,799)

J. HERBERT STEWART
1'40"937 (197,660)
(3)

R. BARRICHELLO STEWART
1'41"351 (196,853)

A. WURZ BENETTON
1'41"444 (196,672)
(4)

R. SCHUMACHER WILLIAMS
1'41"558 (196,451)

D. HILL JORDAN
1'42"050 (195,504)
(5)

J. VILLENEUVE BAR
1'42"087 (195,433)

G. FISICHELLA BENETTON
1'42"110 (195,389)
(6)

O. PANIS PROST
1'42"208 (195,202)

R. ZONTA BAR
1'42"310 (195,007)
(7)

H.H. FRENTZEN JORDAN
1'42"380 (194,874)

J. ALESI SAUBER
1'42"522 (194,604)
(8)

A. ZANARDI WILLIAMS
1'42"885 (193,917)

P. DINIZ SAUBER
1'42"933 (193,827)
(9)

J. TRULLI PROST
1'42"948 (193,799)

M. GENE' MINARDI
1'43"563 (192,648)
(10)

P. DE LA ROSA ARROWS
1'43"579 (192,618)

L. BADOER MINARDI
1'44"321 (191,248)
(11)

T. TAKAGI ARROWS
1'44"637 (190,671)

A Grand Prix one week long! On Saturday at the brand-new Sepang circuit, the two Ferraris amazed the world with the ease with which they conquered the front row. Schumacher was more than one second faster than the two McLarens on his return behind the wheel. Sunday raceday saw a perfect start by Schumacher who powered away followed by Irvine. He then let the Ulsterman pass on lap 4 and proceeded to control Hakkinen. This was the first point of controversy, but more of that later. With the exception of the pit-stops and the accompanying changes in the standings, the race continued without any major surprises. The Ferraris were lapping like clockwork. Coulthard, after a perfect attack on Schuey, went after Irvine but had to stop when he lost fuel pressure on lap 14. Hakkinen tried, without much conviction, to trouble Schumacher but this time nothing could be done against the Ferrari. The chequered flag came down on the two red cars which crossed the finishing line in a triumphant parade. Hakkinen was third followed by Herbert and Barrichello in the Stewarts, Frentzen and Alesi, the local crowd's favourite in the Sauber Petronas.

It was 9.30 European time and they were all celebrating on the Ferrari pit-wall. The cars went to post-race scrutineering and the riders climbed onto the podium for the winners' ceremony. The cold shower came at 11.30 when Jo Bauer, FIA Technical Delegate, announced that the two Ferraris were illegal: the side deflectors (or barge-boards) did not comply with the rules by one centimetre. An FIA release was issued at 12.50. The Ferraris were disqualified and Hakkinen was mathematically world champion, together with McLaren. Ferrari appealed, thus giving rise to one of the longest weeks ever for fans of the Prancing Horse team. Discussion, suspicion and conjecture abounded! How come Hakkinen never complained about Schuey's slowing-down tactics? How come everyone in McLaren was pretty serene as soon as the race was over? Had someone known about Ferrari's 'oversight' for some time and were they preparing to tip off the authorities? The final verdict was issued the following Saturday in Paris. The disqualification was overturned, Ferrari was acquitted, Irvine and Schumacher reinstated and the Ulsterman was back in the lead of the championship by four points over Hakkinen, with everything to play for. See you in Suzuka!

RESULTS

	DRIVER	CAR	KPH	GAP
1	E. Irvine	Ferrari	192.682	-
2	M. Schumacher	Ferrari	192.647	1"040
3	M. Hakkinen	McLaren	192.359	9"743
4	J. Herbert	Stewart	192.101	17"538
5	R. Barrichello	Stewart	191.615	32"296
6	H.H. Frentzen	Jordan	191.530	34"884
7	J. Alesi	Sauber	190.891	54"408
8	A. Wurz	Benetton	190.679	51"191
9	M. Gené	Minardi	188.217	1 lap
10	A. Zanardi	Williams	187.368	1 lap
11	G. Fisichella	Benetton	176.003	4 lap

RETIREMENTS

DRIVER	CAR	LAP	REASON
D. Hill	Jordan	0	Spun off
J. Trulli	Prost	0	Engine
O. Panis	Prost	5	Engine
R. Zonta	Bar	6	Engine
T. Takagi	Arrows	7	Axle-shaft
R. Schumacher	Williams	7	Spun off
D. Coulthard	McLaren	14	Fuel pressure
L. Badoer	Minardi	15	Retirement
P. De La Rosa	Arrows	30	Engine
P. Diniz	Sauber	44	Spun off
J. Villeneuve	Bar	48	Hydraulic circuit

TOPSPEED

DRIVER	MAX.
Hakkinen	304.200
M.Schumacher	300.700
Barrichello	300.200
Alesi	299.000
Coulthard	299.000
Irvine	298.200
Villeneuve	298.100
Frentzen	296.100
Fisichella	295.500
Diniz	295.400
Zanardi	295.100
Wurz	292.700
De La Rosa	292.600
Takagi	291.600
Zonta	291.500
Gené	290.100
R.Schumacher	289.300
Badoer	288.400
Panis	287.900
Herbert	283.400

Japanese GP

The Circuit

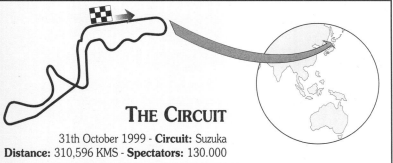

31th October 1999 - **Circuit:** Suzuka
Distance: 310,596 KMS - **Spectators:** 130.000

STARTING GRID

M. Schumacher Ferrari 1'37"470 (216,583) ①	**M. Hakkinen** McLaren 1'37"820
D. Coulthard McLaren 1'38"239 ②	**H.H. Frentzen** Jordan 1'38"696
E. Irvine Ferrari 1'38"975 ③	**O. Panis** Prost 1'39"623
J. Trulli Prost 1'39"644 ④	**J. Herbert** Stewart 1'39"706
R. Schuamcher Williams 1'39"717 ⑤	**J. Alesi** Sauber 1'39"721
J. Villeneuve BAR 1'39"732 ⑥	**D. Hill** Jordan 1'40"140
R. Barrichello Stewart 1'40"140 ⑦	**G. Fisichella** Benetton 1'40"261
A. Wurz Benetton 1'40"303 ⑧	**A. Zanardi** Williams 1'40"403
P. Diniz Sauber 1'40"740 ⑨	**R. Zonta** BAR 1'40"861
T. Takagi Arrows 1'41"067 ⑩	**M. Gene'** Minardi 1'41"529
P. De La Rosa Arrows 1'41"708 ⑪	**L. Badoer** Minardi 1'42"515

The tension and nervousness after Sepang and Paris were evident at the Suzuka circuit on the Saturday before the final race.

The tension between the two teams could almost be cut with a knife and the situation certainly did nothing to help the two protagonists, Hakkinen and Irvine, who both made errors in official qualifying. The driver who benefited the most was Schumacher, who set pole position, becoming favourite for the race. Victory by the German would have meant that Irvine would most probably have become champion. Ferrari strategy therefore was simple: a win for its number 1 driver.

But it was clear that getting a good start at Suzuka was not one of Schumacher's strong points. Instead, Mika got a superb one, shrugged off any attempt at intimidation by Schumacher and powered away from the field with great determination.

Irvine also got off to a good start, overtaking Coulthard who was in front of him on the grid. But the best start came from Panis who found the door left open on the right and blasted through from sixth on the grid to third behind Hakkinen and Schumacher. Mika's lead over the German was soon up to seven seconds and it would virtually stay that way for the rest of the race, demonstrating that the Finn was easily in control; on the other hand, the gap to Irvine was an abyss and the Ulsterman finished the race about one minute behind.

And Coulthard?

From fourth place behind Irvine, he managed to overtake him during the pit-stop, giving the Constructors' title to McLaren. That would have been too much however and 'Lady Luck' took a hand in things, bringing some sense of justice to the championship. First Coulthard had a spin, damaging his nose-cone against the guard-rail and then he stopped for good. Irvine was third and Ferrari won the Constructors' championship, while Hakkinen deservedly took his second successive world title.

Maybe 'Lady Luck' had a name after all: Bernie Ecclestone.

RESULTS

	DRIVER	CAR	KPH	GAP
1	M. Hakkinen	McLaren	204.086	-
2	M. Schumacher	Ferrari	203.899	5"015
3	E. Irvine	Ferrari	200.583	1'35"888
4	H.H. Frentzen	Jordan	200.477	1'38"635
5	R. Schumacher	Williams	200.446	1'39"494
6	J. Alesi	Sauber	199.784	1 lap
7	J. Herbert	Stewart	199.702	1 lap
8	R. Barrichello	Stewart	199.669	1 lap
9	J. Villeneuve	BAR	199.239	1 lap
10	A. Wurz	Benetton	198.907	1 lap
11	P. Diniz	Sauber	198.154	1 lap
12	R. Zonta	BAR	197.161	1 lap
13	P. De La Rosa	Arrows	195.641	2 laps
14	G. Fisichella	Benetton	197.085	7 laps

RETIREMENTS

DRIVER	CAR	LAP	REASON
A. Zanardi	Williams	1	Hydraulic circuit
J. Trulli	Prost	4	Retirement
O. Panis	Prost	20	Engine
D. Hill	Jordan	22	Spunn off
M. Gené	Minardi	32	Gear
D. Coulthard	McLaren	40	Accident
L. Badoer	Minardi	44	Engine
T. Takagi	Arrows	44	Gear

1° - 2° - 3°
1990 N. Piquet - R. Moreno - A. Suzuki
1991 G. Berger - A. Senna - R. Patrese
1992 R. Patrese - G. Berger - M. Brundle
1993 A. Senna - A. Prost - M. Hakkinen
1994 D. Hill - M. Schumacher - J. Alesi
1995 M. Schumacher - Hakkinen - Herbert
1996 D. Hill - M. Schumacher - M. Hakkinen
1997 M. Schumacher - H. Frentzen - E. Irvine
1998 M. Hakkinen - E. Irvine - D. Coulthard

M. Hakkinen (FIN) - McLaren
Ferrari

World Champions 1950-1999

Driver	Team	Year	Constructor
N. Farina	(I - Alfa Romeo)	1950	
J.M. Fangio	(RA - Alfa Romeo)	1951	
A. Ascari	(I - Ferrari)	1952	
A. Ascari	(I - Ferrari)	1953	
J.M. Fangio	(RA - Maserati, Mercedes)	1954	
J.M. Fangio	(RA - Mercedes)	1955	
J.M. Fangio	(RA - Ferrari)	1956	
J.M. Fangio	(RA - Maserati)	1957	
M. Hawthorn	(GB - Ferrari)	1958	Vanwall
J. Brabham	(AUS - Cooper)	1959	Cooper
J. BrabhaM	(AUS - Cooper)	1960	Cooper
P. Hill	(USA - Ferrari)	1961	Ferrari
G. Hill	(GB - Brm)	1962	Brm
J. Clark	(GB - Lotus)	1963	Lotus
J. Surtees	(GB - Ferrari)	1964	Ferrari
J. Clark	(GB - Lotus)	1965	Lotus
J. Brabham	(AUS - Brabham)	1966	Brabham
D. Hulme	(NZ - Brabham)	1967	Brabham
G. Hill	(GB - Lotus)	1968	Lotus
J. Stewart	(GB - Matra)	1969	Matra
J. Rindt	(A - Lotus)	1970	Lotus
J. Stewart	(GB - Tyrrell)	1971	Tyrrell
E. Fittipaldi	(BR - Lotus)	1972	Lotus
J. Stewart	(GB - Tyrrell)	1973	Lotus
E. Fittipaldi	(BR - McLaren)	1974	McLaren
N. Lauda	(A - Ferrari)	1975	Ferrari
J. Hunt	(GB - McLaren)	1976	Ferrari
N. Lauda	(A - Ferrari)	1977	Ferrari
M. Andretti	(USA - Lotus)	1978	Lotus
J. Scheckter	(ZA - Ferrari)	1979	Ferrari
A. Jones	(AUS - Williams)	1980	Williams
N. Piquet	(BR - Brabham)	1981	Williams
K. Rosberg	(SF - Williams)	1982	Ferrari
N. Piquet	(BR - Brabham)	1983	Ferrari
N. Lauda	(A - McLaren)	1984	McLaren
A. Prost	(F - McLaren)	1985	McLaren
A. Prost	(F - McLaren)	1986	Williams
N. Piquet	(BR - Williams)	1987	Williams
A. Senna	(BR - McLaren)	1988	McLaren
A. Prost	(F - McLaren)	1989	McLaren
A. Senna	(BR - McLaren)	1990	McLaren
A. Senna	(BR - McLaren)	1991	McLaren
N. Mansell	(GB - Williams)	1992	Williams
A. Prost	(F - Williams)	1993	Williams
M. Schumacher	(D - Benetton)	1994	Williams
M. Schumacher	(D - Benetton)	1995	Benetton
D. Hill	(GB - Williams)	1996	Williams
J. Villeneuve	(CDN - Williams)	1997	Williams
M. Hakkinen	(FIN - McLaren)	1998	McLaren
M. Hakkinen	(FIN - McLaren)	1999	Ferrari

1999 World Championship : Drivers & Constructors

Drivers	Australian GP	Brazilian GP	San Marino GP	Monaco GP	Spanish GP	Canadian GP	French GP	British GP	Austrian GP	German GP	Hungarian GP	Belgian GP	Italian GP	Europe GP	Malaysia GP	Japanese GP	TOTAL POINTS
Hakkinen	-	10	-	4	10	10	6	-	4	-	10	6	-	2	4	10	76
Irvine	10	2	-	6	3	4	1	6	10	10	4	3	1	-	10	4	74
Frentzen	6	4	-	3	-	-	10	3	3	4	3	4	10	-	1	3	54
Coulthard	-	-	6	-	6	-	-	10	6	2	6	10	2	-	-	-	48
Schumacher M.	-	6	10	10	4	-	2	-	-	-	-	-	-	-	6	6	44
Schumacher R.	4	3	-	-	2	3	3	4	-	3	-	2	6	3	-	2	35
Barrichello	2	-	4	-	-	-	4	-	-	2	-	3	4	2	-	-	21
Herbert	-	-	-	-	-	2	-	-	-	-	-	-	-	10	3	-	15
Fisichella	3	-	2	2	-	6	-	-	-	-	-	-	-	-	-	-	13
Salo	-	-	-	-	-	-	-	-	6	-	-	4	-	-	-	-	10
Hill	-	-	3	-	-	-	-	2	-	-	1	1	-	-	-	-	7
Trulli	-	-	-	-	1	-	-	-	-	-	-	-	-	6	-	-	7
Diniz	-	-	-	-	-	1	-	1	1	-	-	-	-	-	-	-	3
Wurz	-	-	-	1	-	-	-	-	2	-	-	-	-	-	-	-	3
Panis	-	1	-	-	-	-	-	-	-	1	-	-	-	-	-	-	2
Alesi	-	1	-	-	-	-	-	-	-	-	-	-	-	-	1	2
Gené	-	-	-	-	-	-	-	-	-	-	-	-	-	1	-	-	1
De La Rosa	1	-	-	-	-	-	-	-	-	-	-	-	-	-	-	-	1

Constructors

Constructors	Australian GP	Brazilian GP	San Marino GP	Monaco GP	Spanish GP	Canadian GP	French GP	British GP	Austrian GP	German GP	Hungarian GP	Belgian GP	Italian GP	Europe GP	Malaysia GP	Japanese GP	TOTAL POINTS
Ferrari	10	8	10	16	7	4	3	6	10	16	4	3	5	-	16	10	128
McLaren	-	10	6	4	16	10	6	10	10	2	16	16	2	2	4	10	124
Jordan	6	4	3	3	-	-	10	5	3	4	4	5	10	-	1	3	61
Stewart	2	-	4	-	-	2	4	-	-	2	-	3	14	5	-	-	36
Williams	4	3	-	-	2	3	3	4	-	3	-	2	6	3	-	2	35
Benetton	3	-	2	3	-	6	-	-	2	-	-	-	-	-	-	-	16
Prost	-	1	-	1	-	-	-	-	1	-	-	-	-	6	-	-	9
Sauber	-	-	1	-	1	-	1	1	1	-	-	-	-	-	-	1	5
Minardi	-	-	-	-	-	-	-	-	-	-	-	-	-	-	1	-	1
Arrows	1	-	-	-	-	-	-	-	-	-	-	-	-	-	-	-	1

1999 World Championship in brief

	POLE POSITION	WINS	RETIREMENTS	FAST LAPS IN RACE
M. Hakkinen	11	5	5	6
E. Irvine	-	4	1	1
H.H. Frentzen	1	2	3	-
D. Coulthard	-	2	7	3
M. Schumacher	3	2	-	5
R. Schumacher	-	-	4	1
R. Barrichello	1	-	4	-
J. Herbert	-	1	7	-